Legally Kidnapped:

The Case Against Child Protective Services

Carlos Morales

CARLOS MORALES

Acknowledgments

For my mother and father, whose support and virtue have propelled me to seek truth.

I would like to thank those who contribute to Child Protective Services Victim Support, the listeners of the *Truth Over Comfort* podcast, and Linda Jo Martin of www.fightcps.com for her tireless work to help families throughout the country.

Thanks also to the editors of this publication, Calvin Thompson and Cheryl Hulseapple.

If you would like to donate to Child Protective Services Victim support, or if you are in need of advice, please go to cpsvictimsupport.com/contact-us.

Legal Disclaimer

The materials presented in section two of this publication are a culmination of general information, legal documentation, interviews with attorneys and judges, and personal experiences with Child Protective Services and family court. They are not meant to be taken as legal advice. Please contact an attorney if you are taken to court.

About the Author

Carlos Morales is a former Child Protective Services investigator, the president and founder of Child Protective Services Victim Support, the host of the *Truth Over Comfort* podcast, and a committed legal advocate for family reunification.

Since leaving his career as an investigator, he has actively helped families throughout the country fight for their children in and out of court. His pursuit of a radical overhaul for child protection programs has taken him from university lecture halls, to television and radio studios, and finally into the pages of a variety of publications as an author.

TABLE OF CONTENTS

Foreword:
Outside The System
By Brett Veinotte

After spending over a decade in the fields erroneously referred to as education and social services, I managed to fail my way into happiness. And after accumulating my long list of professional failures, I retreated from the system with the following lessons:

- most people have the best of intentions
- unfortunately, the good intentions of the many often enable the corruption of the few
- it is virtually impossible to fight corruption from inside the system, because the well-intentioned people have no power there
- if you really want to help children, work outside the system

During my tenure in state-funded boarding schools and on the periphery of the public education system, I also learned that well-intentioned people are extremely useful in corrupt organizations. We can attend to the logistics, meet quotas, sit attentively through staff meetings and move stacks of paperwork from in-boxes to out-boxes. In fact, with the right training, we seem capable of almost anything outside of asking relevant questions about the corruption or failure itself. That's why a book like Legally Kidnapped can have such a great impact. If capable and well-intentioned people were able to arm themselves with more facts, imagine what a better world they could help to build.

I met this book's author, Carlos Morales, in the summer of 2013. It was a few months after he left his job with CPS and we quickly bonded over a common experience. Although we had traveled our own unique paths through different professions, we both came to the same unsettling realization: despite our aspirations to help young people, we had each naively served institutions and systems that hurt too many of them. While my awakening was slow and often tedious, Carlos' revelations were fast and intense. His book reflects that; it moves swiftly and hits all its targets. It offers a concise and practical examination of one of the least questioned and consequently most corrupt "social services" operations in the country, while elucidating everything from the overarching mission of CPS to the steps to take if an investigator suddenly shows up at your door. Because Legally Kidnapped is short and focused, I wish to add to it a personal account. My story maps the evolution of a worker in a deeply corrupted field, charting the path from naive, obedient and well-intentioned entry-level employee to confident and inquisitive professional who ultimately took positive action. I share it here and elsewhere in the hopes that more people will choose to walk a similar path.

When I first read Carlos' accounts about his time with CPS, I was immediately transported back to the early days of my career. This was a difficult experience; even years after I had left the toughest parts that career behind, I was still haunted by some of the things I saw, many actions I took, the psychiatric drugs I handed out and the numerous opportunities for peaceful solutions I missed. I was angered by the realization that children were merely products we were warehousing, and that they were often further damaged by previous family court and CPS interventions. In the first chapter of Legally Kidnapped Carlos writes, "In investigating my own role within CPS, it's hard not to get emotional. Emotions are not enough, but they do propel me to move forward in my search for truth." I wanted to add some detail about the emotional costs of social service work. These costs extend beyond the consequences of raising questions and speaking out in organizations that resist having certain layers peeled back. The work itself is deeply emotional, for those who care about the people they supposedly serve.

Because of the stories in this book, many readers may come to regard CPS investigators and bureaucrats as malicious or thoughtless, but most social service workers had noble intentions before the system wore them down. When I began my ill-fated social service career in the year 2000, I was fresh out of college and overflowing with idealistic visions and passion. I was so eager to relish the positive differences I could make in the lives of adolescents. I was going to teach; my professional path seemed so straight and clear.

Strangely enough, I spent most of the next decade learning my way out of one job after another. No matter how challenging and enjoyable a position seemed at first, my observations, questions and subsequent realizations would eventually destroy my enthusiasm and willingness to continue. This frustrating process repeated for me in virtually every new station around the public and semi-private schooling system, and I tried numerous stations - boarding school residential counselor, dorm supervisor, outdoor educator, teacher's assistant, behavior manager, lead teacher, history teacher, academic tutor, No Child Left Behind Tutor, SAT group instructor, college consultant. By 2009, while serving as the Vice President of a tutoring company, I finally accepted that I was never going to find lasting satisfaction and enjoyment in the "education" profession, if I had to continue working on the "education" profession's terms.

Was something wrong with me? Could I have ADD or Oppositional Defiant Disorder? After all, if I could not placidly adjust myself to the existing system I must be stricken with some personal defect or dysfunction. At least, that was how I had been trained to view the children under my care. It couldn't have been a problem with the system itself. Most of us have learned that destructive lesson, in school or elsewhere. Yet, upon much reflection, I eventually realized that my experience working in private and around public schools had actually taught me a much more definitive and meaningful lesson. The unfortunate truth was that many of society's systems and institutions are deeply dysfunctional, largely due to a professional failure to question them from within.

In my first teaching position, I remember feeling troubled by my discovery that many of our educational and therapeutic practices were alarmingly suboptimal. I remember feeling vexed and inconvenienced by the frequent notion I should probably change careers. I remember feeling saddened and ultimately infuriated by the conclusion that I had been working against the real educational interests of young people. But above all, I remember feeling diminished by the almost unanimous supervisor and peer reactions to my questions and concerns: annoyance and contempt. At first, I was naive enough to be surprised there was no reward for taking such initiative. After all, I had identified specific, solvable problems and I wanted to explore better methods of helping the young people in our care. Why weren't the middle managers and administrators interested or appreciative? Why was I the one soul with questions and concerns? Why was everyone else tacitly conforming to this anti-educational mayhem we called a school?

Many years later, I started to find some answers to those questions. In 2007, I began an intensive process of reflection, in an effort to make sense of my disconcerting professional experiences. I studied the history of and founding ideologies behind government-run and regulated schooling. I asked questions about nature of that government and its ability to solve complex social problems. I started gathering some disturbing facts, which eventually led me to start recording and editing these investigations and reflections. Within a year, they transformed into the most satisfying educational work I've ever done, the School Sucks Podcast. While the moniker has offended a few people, "school sucks" is actually a very astute synopsis of the system, and one that accurately encompassed the answers to many of my questions. When people first enter school they are curious, innovative, individualistic, creative and optimistic. Yet, twelve years later, for far too many, those essential qualities have either dwindled or been completely sucked away. School has seemingly replaced those natural abilities with conformity, obedience, apathy and a crippling fear of failure.

Then, as the finished products of this schooling process, people go on to staff positions in social services, education, law enforcement and the corporate world. Most are quite comfortable commiserating with co-workers about the finite and mundane burdens of their jobs, but they don't ask meaningful questions about the overall nature and purpose of their work. They have been thoroughly trained to simply go with the flow, which also makes anyone who doesn't acquiesce appear dangerously maladjusted by comparison. In the social services and in education, there are plenty of people who are capable of recognizing problems and then desiring solutions, but it's usually a quiet and personal process, often interrupted and terminated by denial or rationalization. They say things like:

"If I want to change the system, I must work within the system."

This is such a pernicious declaration for the individual – the insistence that each of us must remain subsumed by the collective. This declaration, when repeated with great frequency by enough people, actually ensures a corrupt system's continuity and survival. You can change government and quasi-governmental agencies and systems from within about as successfully as you can tame a lion after it eats you, and any meaningful change from inside is usually ephemeral. These systems are designed to maintain an equilibrium for the powerful interests they've come to benefit – unions, service contractors, corporations and politicians in the case of the schools. Such reform efforts ensure great personal sacrifice, stress, frustration and eventual failure. For those of us who care about helping children, or people in general, we must recognize that the existing government "service" structures have not been set up, maintained or expanded with any of us in mind.

Furthermore, considering the powers potential change agents face, they would be wise to ask themselves, "how small and ineffective do I want to feel? And how long can I endure that feeling?" Eventually the work-within-the-system edict leads most of these idealists to feel worn down and powerless. They will soon realize it's time to give up and begrudgingly accept the status quo.

From my observations, this process usually doesn't take very long. In 2002, I entered graduate school to pursue a Masters degree in something called educational leadership (or public school bureaucracy management if you wish to avoid euphemisms). I sat in classrooms with young men and women who had recently begun their public school teaching careers, and I learned more from these novice teachers than I did from any professor. They collectively taught me a devastating lesson: the public schooling system sucks (professional autonomy, motivation, and self-esteem away) and we all need to reevaluate our childlike enthusiasm for teaching. That isn't a quote, but it seemed to be an ever-present subtext of our class discussions. They also taught me that the work was more about professional survival than it was about student enrichment. Most of my grad school peers had been teaching for 2 or 3 years. That's it. That's all the time it took to transform most of them from passionate idealists to world-weary realists. Despite their frequent complains about the system, they were all there to earn their Masters degrees, which was a requirement to continue working as teachers in that same onerous system. There were seemingly no alternatives left for these once-ambitious souls.

After a couple months of growing despondence, I finally accepted the only lesson I can remember learning in those college classrooms - public schools were torturous environments and teaching in one wasn't for me - and I dropped out. Believing I had cleverly escaped the old work-within-the-system trap, I decided to make the most of the private school teaching job I had at the time.

"This environment is certainly free of the impediment and intransigence of the public system," I reassured myself.

Dissatisfied with the curriculum, injunctions and student-staff interactions in the program I ran, I set out to reform all of it. Despite the almost unanimous supervisor and peer annoyance and contempt that I mentioned earlier, I developed a new curriculum based on life skills and consumer economics, I rewrote the school rules with clinical supervision, and I launched the first school-wide newspaper with my students as the writers, editors and photographers. By in large, the students embraced the new school experience. The other teachers, administrators and students appreciated the newspaper. After two years I was offered a better job within the same organization. It this was the only time in my career that I moved on to a new station with enthusiasm for and satisfaction with what I was leaving behind; I had successfully changed a very small system from the inside!

About six months later, I checked in on my old campus. The newspaper had been discontinued due to "lack of staff interest." The old forbidding rules had all returned. Student-staff relations had deteriorated. The more empowering and appropriate life skills curriculum had been abandoned. Every aspect of the program had reverted back to what was most convenient for those in charge. It was my fault because I hadn't set up or communicated any maintenance plan; I was naïve enough to think it would just continue. In the end, it was like I was never there.

So what was the end result of four years of working my way up to a position where I thought I could have impact? An overwhelming feeling of powerlessness, failure and dejection. I chose to share this one frustrating experience over many others, as it sums up the careers of so many ambitious social service workers - a seemingly ongoing collision between initiative and inertia. However, it was a powerful lesson and a crucial turning point. With a clear understanding of the schooling terrain, I began cutting the path to the truly satisfying educational work I spoke of earlier. It was 2004 and I had compiled a list of priorities that translated an exciting new professional mission:

- Reduce stress.
- Find autonomy and independence.
- Exercise creativity.
- Identify and follow my passions.

- Escape bureaucracy.
- Stop participating in the problem and start helping others.

The problem was these directives - if followed absolutely - left nowhere for me to work. And it was that lack of opportunity that turned out to be a blessing in disguise; the circumstances forced me to recognize that even though I couldn't change the system, I could survive and escape it. And I could probably teach others how to do the same. It was the perfect job description for me, but it was a description for a job that didn't exist. So I started to create it, at first by accident, and ultimately through a long process of trial and error.

By 2011, I was getting paid to produce audio and video content on critical thinking, emotional intelligence, productivity, communication, peaceful parenting and a wide range of historical topics. I had refined my mission: to reclaim that word "education" from those who used institutionalized schools to mold impressionable minds, and to present education as a life-long journey by the individual, for the individual. That small podcast with the word "sucks" in the title, had grown into a flourishing on-line community.

Two years later, I was finally free of all restraints of the schooling system, while still able to do the one thing I had been so passionate about for so long – teach. Today I still operate on the belief that most people capable and well-intentioned, and I aim to share with them information, skills and strategies they can use to build a better world for themselves and others. On a weekly basis, I am able to provide real educational content because I am not under the control of any system or bureaucracy. I am able to maintain control, motivation and enthusiasm for what I teach. The project has now reached hundreds of thousands of people, and it has made a substantial positive impact on the lives of students, parents and even some teachers. I am encouraged knowing that every time I add a new post to my website I reach as many people in a day as I could have reached in about thirty years of teaching in the system. It has been a dramatic evolution from powerlessness and dejection to freedom and tranquility in just five short years.

I have presented my experience here as a success story, but is that really objective? Most education or social services professionals would read these accounts or my resume and only see someone who failed at almost everything. Failure to follow the system's rules. Failure to be a good employee. Failure to be a good graduate student. Failure to be a team player. And the truth is that I was not a visionary. I was not guided by integrity. I was just really lazy about doing things that felt wrong. At the time, most of these failures were quite painful and frustrating, but in retrospect, I wish more professionals could learn to be less afraid of this type of failure.

Please keep my story in mind as you read Legally Kidnapped. If you're discouraged by what you learn about the system, we assure there is always another way to address a significant problem. If you feel small and powerless, remember that supportive networks are available and new ones are being built. If I had not failed my way into the School Sucks Project, I never would have met Carlos Morales. We wouldn't have been able to share ideas, collaborate or offer each other support. Carlos came to our community in 2012, and he quickly impressed me with how he was able to leverage his experience to assist people across the country. His efforts, this book included, exemplify the expanding influence I hoped alternative education could have.

If you read this book as a skeptic or critic of government systems, remember all of the concerned voices in the system being silenced on a regular basis. Think of all the others who might lose sleep at night over what they do, but don't know to effectively speak out. Almost every teacher, every police officer or CPS investigator experiences some of the sentiments I've expressed here. Many have concerns, doubts, frustrations, or even a quiet opposition to the systems they serve. Please remember to honor the rare few who have the courage to speak out.

If you read this book as a worker in education, law enforcement or social services, I encourage you to look for ways to take control and ownership of your life. I encourage you to strive for freedom and satisfaction in your work. The opportunities are out there. If not, they can be created.

If you read this book as someone currently trapped in the CPS system, thank you for taking the time to educate and empower yourself. The world needs more people like you.

Introduction

Humanity knows no bounds to its inhumanity when it puts systems in place that justify its injustices.

Legally Kidnapped: The Case Against Child Protective Services is a radical book. It seeks to strike the root of the problem of child abuse, rather than settling for compromise. This book is a journey inside an agency that has carelessly and often unnecessarily disrupted families throughout the country. With over 400,000 children in the United States currently in the custody of Child Protective Services (CPS), it is imperative that we explore the true intentions and motives behind the organization's work (1). This is a book about CPS, written by a former CPS investigator. I have worked to expose the agency, and I dedicate this book to the past, present, and future victims of CPS—the agency that hurts parents and children time and time again. Though my views may seem extreme, I've backed the information by facts and experience.

After working for the agency and observing the miscalculations and overt corruption, I've found it necessary to expose the exploitative actions carried out in the name of "helping children." Because we do live in a world where parents abuse their children, it is imperative to acknowledge that the agency tasked with protecting these children has failed.

There are well-intentioned people who work for CPS, but they can only do so much in an agency with corrupt incentives that prevent people from doing truly beneficial work. The sad fact is that sexual, emotional, and physical abuse have been rampant in the very foster homes and out-of-home care environments that were created to ensure the safety of children (2). When we lay out all the details, it is abundantly clear that the world would be better off without CPS. Therefore, it is important for families to know how to fight the agency in order to protect their children. To fight the system, you must understand the system, and by reading this book, you will find out the truth about Child Protective Services.

Part 1
The Truth About Child Protective Services

My name is Carlos Morales. I am a former investigator for Child Protective Services, and I am guilty. I'm guilty of what many American citizens are guilty of—the belief that CPS has the child's best interest in mind. I'm guilty of working for an organization that commits atrocity after atrocity, hampers freedom throughout the United States, and causes millions of parents to live in fear. I'm guilty of working for an organization that has done more to carry out the War on Drugs than the War Against Child Abuse. I'm guilty of working for an agency that has essentially kidnapped children, thrown them into foster homes, and destroyed their lives. I'm guilty of working for CPS.

As an investigator for CPS, I did not help children; I hurt them. I did not protect families; I helped ruin them. I did not work to benefit society; I helped corrupt it. CPS damages and controls society from within, by allowing the state to take over the lives of children. As retired Supreme Court Judge Bryan Lindsey put it, "There is no system ever devised by mankind that is guaranteed to rip husband and wife or father, mother and child apart so bitterly than our present Family Court System."

When I began to examine CPS, I realized I was looking at an agency that existed in direct opposition to my first allegiance—the protection of the most underprivileged and abused minority in the world: children. In investigating my own role within CPS, it's hard not to get emotional. Emotions are not enough, but they do propel me to move forward in my search for truth.

Truth is not about comfort, and it is not about ignoring what exists right in front of our eyes. Motive, intent, and best interest matter very little to truth. Those with the greatest of intentions can commit the greatest of atrocities, and it is those noble intentions that have created many of our current social, political, and economic ills.

19

"Of all tyrannies, a tyranny sincerely exercised for the good of its victims may be the most oppressive. It would be better to live under robber barons than under omnipotent moral busybodies. The robber baron's cruelty may sometimes sleep, his cupidity may at some point be satiated; but those who torment us for our own good will torment us without end for they do so with the approval of their own conscience."
—*C.S. Lewis*

With a belief in the goodness of people, I offer the facts regarding CPS. You can do what you like with these facts, but to ignore them for the sake of comfort is to turn your back on what is right. From the horrific effects of foster homes, to the financial incentives to remove children from their parents, from the Drug War that is pushed forward more by CPS than it is by the DEA (Drug Enforcement Agency), to the destruction of families—the good intentions of caseworkers cannot repel these bad consequences of a system that does very little to help those who need it the most.

What Is Child Protective Services?

Child Protective Services (CPS) is the name of the U.S. government agency that responds to reports of child abuse or neglect (3). Not every state calls this agency CPS. Other names include the "Department of Children and Family Services," the "Department of Social Services," the "Department of Children, Youth, and Family Services," "Social Services," etc. Though there are many different monikers and slightly different laws, depending on the state, the nature of the agency is the same.

The agency was founded based upon an idea and legal term created in 1696, called *parens patriae,* which is Latin for "parent of the nation." It gives the royal crown—the government—care of all "charities, infants, idiots, and lunatics returned to the chancery" (4).

In the United States, it wasn't until 1825 that the government enacted laws that gave social-welfare agencies the right to remove neglected children from their parents. The first true foster homes in the U.S. weren't created until the Children's Aid Society (CAS) was created in 1853. CAS removed children from their homes and sent them to become indentured servants for farming families.

Then in 1909, Theodore Roosevelt created agovernment funded volunteer organization that would "establish and publicize standards of child care" (5).

Throughout history, adults have treated children as less than second-class citizens. Calling children's lives "slave labor" is putting it lightly. From the history of infanticide by parents in every country until relatively recently, to the barbaric "discipline" practices still on full display today, the history of childcare has been a history of harsh punishment.

Society has made remarkable strides in childcare over the last 200 years, in part due to industrialization that has allowed children to move out of slave farming and slave mining, and into less hostile learning environments. It's undeniable that some of the government's tactics benefited some children in the past. In rare cases, they have today as well. But we must grasp the underpinnings of many of the social justice agencies in the late 18th and early 19th centuries in order understand what the agency has become. The progressive intentions of these initial government programs, which campaigned for the "protection of the unprotected," were far from ideal.

In the early 19th century, after a boom in the economy and an influx of immigration into the United States, the American and British aristocracy became outraged by the influx of "savages" moving to, and being born in, the U.S. "Savages" were defined as those who did not share the same values as the white puritanical aristocracy. This group included Native Americans, Africans, Hispanics, and even the Irish. This marked the beginning of what we now know as "progressivism" (6).

Today, many view progressivism as a way forward to a brighter future, but this does not reflect its history. Progressivism began as the coercive scientific management of humanity by various corporate and state interests to alter the mindset and actions of those they saw as undesirable. It was a form of regression that used force to prevent a new and changing society.

In layman's terms, British and American white aristocrats wanted to ensure that they would be able to retain power. In order to accomplish this, they had to place it under the veneer of science, when it was in fact a pseudoscience. They based this, in part, on the work of

Francis Galton, who was the second cousin of Charles Darwin. Galton, an English Victorian progressive, performed beneficial work in statistical analysis, but his work was later used to statistically analyze the intelligence of those he considered feeble minded.

In his recent book covering the history of the progressivism and eugenics movements, *War Against the Weak: Eugenics and America's Campaign to Create a Master Race,* Edwin Black demonstrates Galton's views and the views of early progressives (7):

> *"Could not the undesirables be got rid of and the desirables multiplied?" [Galton] asked.*

> *. . . He played with many names. . . . Finally, he scrawled Greek letters on a hand-sized scrap of paper, and next to them the two English fragments he would join into one. The Greek word for well was abutted to the Greek word for born . . . The word he wrote on that small piece of paper was eugenics.*

> *. . . Above all, Galton concluded that the caliber of progeny always reflected its distant ancestry. Good lineage did not improve bad blood. On the contrary, in any match, undesirable traits would eventually outweigh desirable qualities. Hence, when eugenically preferred persons mated with one another, their offspring were even more valuable. But mixing eugenically well-endowed humans with inferior mates would not strengthen succeeding generations. Rather, it would promote a downward biological spiral. What was worse, two people of bad blood would only create progressively more defective offspring.*

> *. . . Galton asserted, ". . . by means of isolation, or some other drastic yet adequate measure, a stop should be put to the production of families of children likely to include degenerates."*

With the help of the U.S. government, they decided upon a solution to the "problems" of the booming population, immigration, and the fear of the destruction of "good lineage." They did this through the codification, ostracism, and annihilation of those who were considered unfit. This view was well regarded in schools and universities across the United States. Again, to quote *War Against the Weak:*

> *By 1914, some forty-four major institutions offered eugenic instruction. Within a decade, that number would swell to hundreds, reaching some 20,000 students annually. High schools quickly adopted eugenic textbooks as well.*

> *Proponents of this eugenics plan were financed by the Carnegie Group and other high ranking business owners and politicians. The plan was to lower the numbers of the unfit, and one way of accomplishing this was through forced sterilization. In just over 70 years, the United States sterilized over 100,000 individuals. They chose these people based on race, IQ, cultural heritage, and/or "proclivity toward criminality" based on skull shape. This process involved policemen going into people's homes, kidnapping children, and forcibly sterilizing them—many died during these sterilizations.*

> *The Western State Hospital in Virginia was notable in its "accomplishments" in lowering population numbers, though other facilities in Virginia and across the country took action to sterilize as well (7).*

Western State Hospital in Staunton was not Virginia's only sterilization mill. Others dotted the state's map, including the Colony for Epileptics and the Feebleminded near Lynchburg, which was the nation's largest facility of its kind and the state's greatest center of sterilization. Western and Lynchburg were augmented by hospitals at Petersburg, Williamsburg, and Marion. Lower-class white boys and girls from the mountains, from the outskirts of small towns and big city slums, were sterilized in assembly line fashion. So were American Indians, blacks, epileptics, and those suffering from certain maladies— day after day, thousands of them, as though orchestrated by some giant machine.

Retired Montgomery County Welfare Director Kate Bolton recalled with pride, "The children were legally committed by the court for being feebleminded, and there was a waiting list from here to Lynchburg." She added, "If you've seen as much suffering and depravity as I have, you can only hope and pray no one else goes through something like that. We had to stop it at the root."

The Supreme Court upheld these practices, with Justice Oliver Wendell Holmes pronouncing a need for eugenics in order to save society:

> *It is better for all the world, if instead of wanting to execute degenerate offspring for crime, or let them starve for their imbecility, society can prevent those who are manifestly unfit from continuing their kind. The principle that sustains compulsory vaccination is broad enough to cover cutting the Fallopian tubes. Three generations of imbeciles is enough.*

This was a common practice throughout the United States, and the parameters that determined who was "unfit" became entirely subjective. Social welfare agents in North Carolina, up until 1974, were granted the power to forcibly sterilize anyone they saw as unfit. They did this without any form of objective testing. They targeted black families in the majority of these cases.

They also regularly targeted Native American tribes, not only for sterilization, but also for the removal of children from their homes. Children were placed outside of their tribes based on the whims of social workers, and they were put into white foster homes and white public schools (8).

In response to this epidemic, the Indian Child Welfare Act was passed in 1978. This put restrictions on social worker's abilities to take children out of their home tribes (9). This also lowered the horrendous practice of sterilizing Native American mothers, who were threatened with having their children removed if they did not "voluntarily" choose to be sterilized.

Prior to this ruling, very few limitations were place upon social workers who wanted to remove children. They viewed anything other than the puritan nuclear family as potentially dangerous for the child. Simply put, any home that contained any more than two parents and two children living in the domicile was considered unsuitable. As a result, immigrants who lived with extended family (grandparents, aunts, uncles, nephews, etc.) in the home were dealt with.

Many of the children from these families were placed in white foster homes for re-education, and a great number were sterilized at a young age without their knowledge (7).

Though the forced sterilization of people based on race is not often used within the United States anymore, the removal of children from homes is still heavily tilted toward one particular race—African Americans. According to national data, 37 percent of children in foster care are African American. The racial bias becomes apparent when you realize that African American children make up only 15 percent of the U.S. population (10).

In truth, the majority of CPS investigators and workers are not aware of the eugenics and anti-immigration-based history of CPS. Nevertheless, the practices seen within the bureaucracies, state management, and foster homes of today are not much better than those of CPS's beginnings.

Part 2
A Culture of Fear

"Fear obscures reason, intensifies emotions and makes it easier for demagogic politicians to mobilize the public on behalf of the policies they want to pursue."
—Former U.S. National Security Advisor Zbigniew Brzezinski (11)

"I doubt there has ever been a human culture, anywhere, anytime, that underestimates children's abilities more than we North Americans do today."
—Boston College Psychology Professor Emeritus Peter Gray

Within the United States, 68 percent of Americans believe that there should be a law that prohibits children age nine and under from being allowed to play unsupervised at a park. Forty-three percent of those polled felt the same way about twelve-year-olds (12). To put this in context, these people would find it fit to criminalize all preteenagers who played outside without a parent by their side. The parent could also be held liable and could end up being arrested. How it benefits a child to have a parent thrown in jail is beyond understanding; people often throw rationality out the window in a quest for punishment.

Laws mean very little when no one supports them. This is why very few people are arrested for jaywalking in NYC, why no one is arrested for picking up seaweed in New Hampshire (13), and why no one is convicted of cunnilingus in North Carolina, where it is considered a crime against nature (14). In other words, for a law to have any teeth, people must fear not only the repercussions of breaking the law, but also fear others breaking it.

In order for people to back a law, a culture of fear must be created to ensure pseudo-consent. A constant state of fear ensures obedience. When it comes to people's fear regarding children's ability to take care of themselves, or evil men putting their dirty hands on children, the United States has implemented horizontal, peer control through manipulation. Fear sells in the media, and in government, it creates growth.

The "fear of the other" is integral to the continued growth and range of power that benefits CPS. When I worked for the agency, there were times when I was truly shocked regarding some of the reports coming in. I wasn't shocked because they were horrific acts of abuse; I was shocked by what people considered abuse.

I recall a report that complained a parent was allowing her thirteen-year-old son to ride his bike around the block. I had to interview four neighbors, ten family members, and school personnel in order to close the case. Other reports included children playing with other children in a front yard by themselves, even though the parent was inside the home. Apparently—gasp—the parent may have been napping at the time. Neither my supervisor, nor my colleagues, found these accusations to be as absurd as I did. I recall my supervisor telling me, "While it was fine to play outside when I was a kid, it's not anymore."

She would then cite the rationale for her fear—some bad thing that had happened to a child 1,500 miles away who was playing outside. I was naive, according to my supervisor, and this was why I did not take these "horrifying" situations of neglect more seriously. "What if [the child] were hit by a car?"

CPS workers are not the only ones concerned about the possibility of children playing outside. Without the people who report such cases of "child neglect," there is very little CPS can do. A mother was charged with child neglect and thrown in jail for allowing her son, aged seven, to play outside—something that very few children are allowed do these days. For such charges to happen, first someone has file a report.

The child was half a mile away from his home—about a seven-minute walk—in a park. A stranger walked up to the child and asked him, "Where is your mom?" The man then called the cops, because—why not? The cops then went to the mother's home and strapped handcuffs on the dastardly terrorist-breeding woman, and charged her with child neglect.

Children playing outside is not the only thing that gets people in a tizzy. A woman in Long Island, New York, was arrested for leaving her seven-year-old at the Roosevelt Field Mall Lego Store for over an hour while she shopped in other stores in the same mall (15).

I've helped a few parents deal with these issues since leaving the agency, including a mother who left her children in a van for five minutes while picking up some food to go from a restaurant. It was 70 degrees outside, and a random passerby chose to call the cops. Mind you, the worried accuser did not bother to check on the children, but simply dialed and walked away. Thankfully, the case was thrown out with a bit of help, but not without great distress, wasted time, and children left in fear.

Not everyone in this situation is so "lucky." A Chicago woman was charged with endangering a child's life after leaving her child in a car for—according to the police report—less than five minutes. Paramedics were called to "check on the health of the children" after the "horrific" incident. I wonder when people will start being arrested for sitting in traffic too long without turning the AC on (16).

Sarcasm aside, there are of course issues of neglect in America. There have been a few cases were children were left in their parents' cars for too long, but these cases are very rare. The rarity is never mentioned in the news, though, and when we live in a country of 300 million people, there will always be outliers who act in a terrible manner. When the media bombards us with these rare tragedies, it leads people to view the incidences as the norm.

In fact, children are now safer than ever from being kidnapped by people who are not state officials—in other words, the random child-molesting strangers who all those in the "stranger generation" were told lurked around every corner. In his book *Protecting the Gift,* child-safety expert Gavin De Becker points out that a child is more likely to have a heart attack than be kidnapped by a stranger, but you don't see 24-hour news coverage on CNN of little Johnnie's heart attack.

University of Southern California sociology professor Barry Glassner wrote about missing children in his book *The Culture of Fear:*

> *In national surveys conducted in recent years, 3 out of 4 parents say they fear that their child will be kidnapped by a stranger. They harbor this anxiety, no doubt, because they keep hearing frightening statistics and stories about perverts snatching children off the street. What the public doesn't hear often or clearly enough is that the majority of missing children are runaways fleeing from physically or emotionally abusive parents (17).*

CPS is not alone in sticking children in a position whereby they can be stripped away from their parents permanently for voluntarily choosing to play outside, but CPS's monopolistic power to dictate what is in the "best interest of the child" enforces the fears of society. In actuality, children are more likely to be kidnapped by state workers than by anyone else; the fear of strangers helps lead to these legal kidnappings. We can create a more rational approach to child safety and individual liberty by prioritizing facts above emotions and truth above gut feelings.

Part 3
My Journey

My First Case

Not all cases that I dealt with at CPS were unwarranted. There are situations in which a child should be removed from a home. An example of this was my first case, which I wrote about in one of my early essays about the agency. (I've changed names to protect the innocent.)

There I was standing in children's shit. It was 2012 and I was on my first case on my first day of work for CPS. A call came in that there was a drug raid in the ghettos of San Antonio, Texas. A female investigator—who after several years at the agency had become jaded, aggravated, and lacking in empathy toward anyone's plight—was training me.

Her name was Vanessa, and standing at 5'2", she felt that she needed to play the uncaring strong type in order to get any respect by the supposed parental criminals and child abusers that she worked with day in and day out. Maria Garcia was the name of the woman involved in the case, and she was accused of criminal neglect after living in squalor with her five children—in a house infested with countless drugs and an abhorrent amount of waste.

It was raining and muggy, and while driving toward the scene, I counted four dead cats on the side of the road. Why are poor neighborhoods always littered with dead animals? In front of the home were seven DEA officers and cops and a number of small children, ages ranging from three to ten. A Hispanic woman was on her knees in the driveway. She was in hysterics, with tears rolling down in her cheek. I opened my car door and heard a deep guttural cry that still haunts me. None of the officers paid much attention, and a young one stepped up to Vanessa.

"We've been watching these fuckers for the last couple of weeks," he told her.

Apparently the residents of the house were full-time drug dealers—heroin, cocaine, marijuana, Xanax, oxycodone, etc. The outside of the house was in disrepair, with a few broken lawn chairs in front, a pregnant dog and its dirty pups walking around, and boarded up windows.

The officer explained that drug dealers and buyers regularly came in and out of the home. A Humvee was parked outside the place, with 24-inch rims and a custom paint job. If this belonged to the drug dealer, they were doing quite well. Neighbors throughout the year had repeatedly told cops about constant noise disturbances, horrific yelling, and random men stepping in and out. The DEA officers, armed with a warrant and a plethora of ammunition, had broken into the home in the morning and ripped up the place to find both narcotics and the profits resulting from the drug sales.

"Want to check it out?" The officer asked the question with excitement. He wanted to reveal the seedy underworld to me, the new CPS investigator, since he had been involved in it since his career had started.

I walked into the home. There was an overwhelming stench. None of the lights were on; apparently, the power had been off for the last two months. Windows were boarded up, couches were flipped over due to the intensive DEA search, and there were dozens of empty Keystone Light cans scattered throughout the kitchen and living room. A flat-screen TV was mounted to the wall. I encountered a similar situation in every home I investigated, no matter what the financial situation of the family. All I could think about was the overwhelming stench.

"Check this shit out," the officer said while bringing me to the back room.

The smell got stronger as we opened up the door.

Feces were smeared on the walls and floor, and everything was soaked with urine. There were spots here and there that seemed pristine though.

"The scumbags were telling the kids to urinate and defecate in this room as a deterrent toward anyone wanting to steal their product. When I talked to the kids, they didn't think that there was anything strange about it." He asked, "See those clean spots? That's apparently the safe spots for keeping the product."

I was completely overwhelmed, not only from the scene and smells, or the horrific situation the kids where in, but also by the emotional optimism that the officers and lead CPS investigator seemed to hold. This was consistent throughout my employment with the agency. War stories were a badge of honor and an ego boost, and it wasn't so much about helping others as it was about playing the game.

I hadn't a clue what was to come next. The only thing I thought about was how to get the kids the hell out of here. After surveying a bit more of the home, I walked out of the house with a completely different mindset than when I started work for the first time that day. I had heard stories like this before, but had never seen the depravity firsthand.

Again, I heard the cries of a woman in the driveway. She was Maria Garcia. "Don't take my fucking kids away! I didn't do anything wrong. We didn't even really live there!" The woman was obviously in desperation, and her children surrounded her, trying to put her at ease. Vanessa, the lead investigator, stepped up to the women and stated that she knew the woman was lying.

Maria explained that she had only been at the house for a few days, that they had kidnapped her, and then that she was there on her own volition. She went back and forth with contradicting stories, and between every whimper and tear, she would come up with some other rationalization for why she was there with her children. Maria uttered that she had never even taken any drugs. Vanessa looked at me with a bit of glee, opened up her purse, and pulled out a white package. She opened the package and showed Maria an oral-swab drug test.

"See this thing? This is a drug test. If you haven't taken anything, then this is going to tell me."

Maria seemed very hesitant at this point, and her sadness became anger. She agreed to the drug test, and opened her mouth for the swab. In order for the test to be valid, the alleged drug user has to place a white sponge in their mouth. The sponge is connected to a piece of plastic with a readout on it. Vanessa read the test while the women continued to plea, and low and behold, she tested positive for opiates and cocaine. Vanessa looked pleased at the results; on this test alone you could get a child removal.

"You tested positive for two different types of drugs."

Maria, not looking particularly surprised, began to explain that the drug dealers had forced her to take them. Though at the time I was a trusting person, it was becoming rather obvious that this woman would say anything to keep from losing her kids—and more importantly—to keep herself out of jail.

"You see those boards on the windows? Yeah, they prevented us from getting out," she said.

The young DEA officer stepped in and said he had seen Garcia and the kids outside quite often over the last couple of weeks.

"Well, yeah, but no, you're wrong," replied the mother.

Her ten-year-old child, Stephanie, stepped forward and attempted to back her mother's story. She offered similar contradictions and pleas, so we knew we weren't dealing with someone telling the truth.

Out of the corner of my eye, I saw three Hispanic women running toward the scene. An elderly lady explained that she was the children's grandmother, and she begged us to give her the children.

Vanessa explained to me that there was "no fucking way we were going to give the kids to her," because the grandmother knew that the kids were at the home and didn't do anything about it. The two other women who came with the grandmother explained that the kids would be worse off in a foster home, and that they would be molested, drugged, and abused there.

I shrugged off this assertion, as did Vanessa, though in later research the women's generalizations and accusations regarding foster homes were proven statistically to be true. Vanessa made a call to a judge. All I heard was, "We've got the go-ahead for an exogen [emergency] removal."

We put three of the kids in the back of my car and the two others in Vanessa's. They were crying, and the six-year-old claimed that he was going to run out of the car. Thankfully, I had child-lock on while he attempted to open the door during my drive back to CPS headquarters. We put the children in a white room with a couple of creepy "kid friendly" posters on the wall, some old toys, and stuffed animals.

A large double-paned glass window took over a complete wall, which allowed the investigators to watch cases. I would see this room a lot. We used it for "parent visitation," and I would spy in from the other room to take notes about everything I saw.

Overwhelmed on the first day, I told Vanessa that I needed to use the restroom and asked whether she would watch over the kids. She agreed. I stared at my reflection in the mirror in an isolated bathroom, trying to conceptualize what had just happened. Tears rolled down my eyes, and I had to sit on the floor just to keep myself together. I played everything back in my mind, and attempted to stabilize myself.

After a couple of minutes, I cleaned off my face and walked back into the room. The children had calmed down by this point, and they were taken one by one to a camera-filled room to be interviewed. After three hours, all the interviews were done and I was told that CPS had enough information to "remove the kids for a long time." Another investigator had found a temporary foster home for them. The children were split up, and around midnight, we dropped them off.

This was my first day. This is what sold me on CPS, and this was the most open-and-shut case I ever had. The abuse was clear, and I believed the remedy was a foster home.

I visited the kids a couple days later. Every one of them was now on psychotropic medication, and every one of them missed their mother. The children seemed hazy, and they complained about how they were being treated in the foster home. Vanessa told me that kids always "bitch about foster homes," and it wasn't until later on that I learned just why this was so often the case.

From an outsider's perspective, removals like this prove the importance of CPS. But a more in-depth look into the rampant removal of children for "playing outside," for fighting with other children, and for being raised in "dirty houses" that were determined so based upon dirty pans—while ignoring actual abuse—would make anyone second-guess the positive aspects of CPS.

Throughout my time at the agency, I saw CPS workers place many children in out-of-home care for such reasons, or place them in mental health facilities in order to "deal with their issues." Children were strapped down, drugged, mocked, and institutionalized. We addressed their issues with pharmacology rather than empathy, and through coercion rather than care.

My History

Two years before joining, I never had any desire to work for the government, never mind CPS. I went to university to become a sociologist, and it wasn't until I began to understand the intimate connection between child abuse and abusive adults that I began to gravitate toward working in child welfare.

My parents raised me in an upper-middle class Catholic household, with a doctor father and a stay-at-home mother. In many ways, I came from a place of privilege that was very different from that of the people I helped when I took my first internship, where I worked for a child advocacy nonprofit group, which specialized in investigating sexual molestation cases with the help of CPS.

I spent a couple months working for the nonprofit, where I worked among empathetic and caring employees. The primary purpose of the facility was conducting forensic interviews with children who had allegedly been victims of sexual abuse. Children were taken into a room—generally already having a pending CPS case—where they were asked a variety of questions regarding the sexual behaviors of the people in their lives. Unlike CPS investigators, the interviewer here specialized and went to school for training in interviewing children. CPS investigators would sit in another room while the interview occurred.

Texas was different from other states in dealing with sexual abuse cases. Due to a tendency for investigators to obfuscate and lead children into making sexual abuse allegations, even when untrue (I believed it was subconscious at first)—the Texas branch of CPS worked with the nonprofits that specialized in interviewing children who had allegedly been molested. The nonprofits were properly run and offered victim services, such as counseling and other activities that were funded by various government grants and corporations.

My problem was that the agency wasn't interesting enough for me. I wanted to work as an investigator, someone who stepped in, discovered, and genuinely attempted to prevent the abuse from happening in the first place.

While in college, there had been a number of altercations where I had attempted to stop parents from abusing their children in public. These attempts tended to be not very beneficial to the situation. I once observed a man slapping his three- to four-year-old child across the face in a grocery store because she attempted to grab a balloon that she wanted. She began whimpering and he continuing to scream at her.

In a badly thought-out solution, I put my hands behind my back, got on my knees to come down to the child's level and asked her father, "Does it make you feel like a man to hit a four-year-old girl?"

My hostility led to an exacerbation of his hostility and he threw me on the floor. I got up, saying, "Now do you feel like a man?"

He pushed me again as I got up, and I repeated the phrase. The man yelled and screamed that it was wrong for me to tell him "how to raise his fucking daughter."

During the whole charade, I kept my hands behind my back, as I wanted no one to assume that I was in any way trying to assault the man. When people see a six-foot-two-inch, 200-pound Puerto Rican like me in a hostile situation with an old white man, they will most likely take the older man's side. A manager of the store quickly broke up the situation in order to calm things down. Two elderly women walked up to me and said that I had no right to tell anyone how to raise their kids.

Putting this into context, a four-year-old was slapped in the face and the assaulter was protected. Someone called the cops. The parents of the girl immediately bought her a balloon and a stuffed animal in order to appear like "great parents." Officers questioned me. I explained the situation, and they replied that I should have called CPS. In that moment, I decided that I needed to work for the agency that worked in the trenches. I ended my internship, finished my degree, and sent in my resume.

Part 4
What It Takes to Be a CPS Investigator

The Application Process

To be honest, my resume was weak. I had majored in sociology; I had an internship under my belt, and I had written a few research papers on child development. Nevertheless, CPS accepted it and sent me an application with around 200 questions. These questions were multiple-choice inquiries that were as shallow as a puddle, and organized to weed out rebellious types. After researching these questions—given to potential employees of corporations and governments—I realized that they were trying to catch contradictions. They were also looking for employees who were willing to abide by strict corporate and state standards. I answered while knowing this. Lo and behold, I passed their tests and got an interview.

The human resources head made me aware that I had tested highly and that they were excited about hiring me. She started the interviewing process by going over the tremendous dangers of the job. She discussed not only the stressful conditions that I'd be dealing with, but also the possibility that angry parents could murder me. Disgruntled parents had lit investigators' cars on fire. Others had shot investigators during home visitations, and assault and battery was common. At the time, I thought these warnings were overblown, but after having a gun pointed at me on a few occasions as an investigator, I no longer take that warning lightly.

An interesting statistic presented to me was that 50 percent of CPS investigators in Texas quit within the first year due to stress and anxiety. After working for the agency for just one day, I was surprised that it was only one in two who quit that quickly.

What Is a Child Protective Services Investigator?

According to the Texas Department of Family and Protective Services, a CPS investigator's job is to "investigate allegations of child abuse and neglect." They have the difficult task of figuring out what happened in a given situation, and of predicting what may happen in the future. CPS receives and investigates reports of abuse and neglect twenty-four hours per day, every day of the year.

A CPS investigation involves interviewing and gathering information to see whether abuse or neglect happened, and whether intervention is necessary. The investigator considers both risk and safety issues and may recommend services for the child and family in order to reduce the risk of further abuse or neglect. The purposes of a CPS investigation are to see whether a child can safely live with their family, to find out whether abuse or neglect happened, to learn whether other children in the family are victims of abuse or neglect, to determine whether there is a risk of abuse or neglect in the future, and to develop a plan, if needed, to keep the child or children safe.

In order to strive for success in this position, training is obviously necessary. Training would take two months, two-thirds of which would be conducted in a classroom and one-third in the field.

Training

Placed in a small classroom with other soon-to-be investigators, I understood rather quickly that CPS was willing to take just about anyone. One of my coworkers was a recent college graduate who majored in jazz saxophone. Within two months, this saxophone master would become a full-fledged investigator who had to decipher fact from fiction. He would also have the power to remove a child from their home.

Many of my future coworkers joined because they just needed a job, and CPS was an action-packed place to get one. Outside of joining the police force or military, there are few employers who tell the individuals they hire—and society repeats the message—that they are heroes. CPS tells investigators that they are fighting for those who don't have a voice. They say the short training period investigators receive prepares them to possess a keen understanding of child development.

Without this understanding, how could someone be prepared to properly ask small children questions? Questions that could put them in shock, questions that could lead them to make false allegations, or even questions that could prevent them from coming forward with the truth.

We had to have insights into psychology in order to interpret body language and emotional reactions, and in order to gather evidence from suspected child abusers. To top it off, we also had to have training in dispute resolution, due to the overwhelming stress and hostility that investigators have to deal with. Many times investigators work in impoverished and dangerous neighborhoods. We might accuse parents of drug use, sexual molestation, physical abuse, or a large variety of actions that CPS considers abusive. These accusations could lead to parental hostility, lying, manipulation, or physical violence.

According to the state of Texas at the time, an investigator only needed two months of training to absorb all of this information. In this small amount of time, the state gave us the power to change a family forever.

The majority of my training involved former investigators and supervisors sharing war stories. They were preparing us for a battle of sorts. A battle against "evil" parents, and we were the crusaders who had come to save the innocent children. We believed we were the chosen few who would save society from itself!

Part 5
The Investigation Begins

How a Case Starts

Now that you are aware of the training of the state heroes of the story, let's go into how a CPS investigation starts in most places around the country. Someone calls CPS headquarters to allege abuse. The caller can be anonymous, or they can state their actual name. Due to CPS bylaws, the alleged perpetrator is never given the name. Those knowledgeable regarding the U.S. Constitution may recall that this secrecy in an infringement of the Sixth Amendment, but the state justifies it for the "well-being of the child." In fact, while working for CPS and researching it further, I found that the Fourth, Fifth, Sixth, Seventh, Eighth, and Fourteenth amendments were all ignored in many CPS proceedings.

The alleged abuses may include a parent allowing a child to play outside (18), a parent homeschooling a child (19), or a parent smoking marijuana outside the home, even if the state legally allows smoking (20), but sometimes there is actual abuse. From there, a supervisor reads the report, and sends an investigator to corroborate or disprove the claims.

What you must understand is that according to the U.S. government, a parent does not own the rights to care for their own child. Instead, the true responsibility for childcare belongs to the state. If government workers believe that a parent is not acting in accordance with government rules, then the state can take complete responsibility and control over the child. Because of this, CPS workers may question a child without obtaining parental consent. Such questioning may be done at the child's school, church, community center, or pretty much anywhere. Public (i.e., government) schools are, more often than not, where CPS chooses to perform such investigations. This is due to the fact that "public" schools and government are one and the same, and the education department, like CPS, is a government agency.

Questioning a Child

I am going to create a scenario for you. Pretend you're five years old, and you've just started school. You're new to the culture, and you have not become accustomed to random adults questioning you. The school personnel are also strangers that children are told they have to spend their days with and trust simply because the strangers are school workers. Suddenly, some person you've never met comes into your class. They say that they need to speak to you. The teacher nods her head that it's okay to go.

The person takes you into a room where they ask whether it's okay to record the conversation. (According to CPS, a five-year-old is capable of consent.) They ask personal questions. For instance, what's your favorite color? How do you like school? Who is your favorite teacher? These questions are supposed to help you feel at ease, but this rarely works.

After these vanilla-type questions, the true investigation begins. Some of the questions that follow may play a part in the case, and others are asked for the purpose of filling out assessments. These questions can include, have you ever touched your father's penis? How often do your parents hit you? How many minutes a day are you allowed to play outside? Have you ever seen your parents smoke? Have you ever seen stuff that looks like grass in the house?

What I found was that the child could become quite fearful in these circumstances. In order to appease the investigator and escape the situation, the child would often answer yes or no even if they didn't know the answer. Furthermore, if a question was open-ended, often children would make up stories. This left the investigator the job of picking which part of the contradictory story was true; anything that sounded like it could be abusive could be cherry-picked as valid.

We must call the validity of children's answers into question due to the authoritative nature of these investigations, and due to the wild imaginations of children. Often, children will appease investigators by agreeing or stating "yes" to allegations of abuse. This is a natural result of a child's need to make authority figures happy. In addition, investigators don't want to feel as if they've wasted their time. Instead, they want to feel like heroes. This urge is only natural, but the consequences can be dire. The moral panic about satanic ritual abuse in the 1980s and 1990s provides a fascinating study into this. CPS played a large part in the panic.

Part 6
Satan and the Issue with Evidence

Satanic Ritual Abuse: A Case Study in Stupidity

Satanic ritual abuse (SRA) allegations started after the publication of a since debunked book by the name of *Michelle Remembers.* The authors claimed that several cases of child abuse—abuse that never even happened—were the work of Satanists. The authors then gave SRA training to police officers, CPS investigators, and prosecutors. The training all occurred under the presupposition that Satanists were among us and they were carefully designing new ways of abusing children. The authors consulted authorities in over 1,000 SRA-related cases (21).

This fear of SRA led to a wave of false allegations, due to some very cleverly constructed questions. The most notable case was the McMartin preschool trial. Investigators went to the school in order to question children regarding experiences of alleged sexual molestation, physical abuse, ritualistic sacrifice, and witchcraft by supposedly satanic day-care workers.

The investigators used highly suggestive techniques to coach children into absurd accusations. The questioning tactics included telling children to pretend and to speculate about events. They interviewed several hundred children, out of which 360 alleged that they had been abused. The accusations were made in 1983. The arrests and the pretrial investigation ran from 1984 to 1987, and the trial ran from 1987 to 1990. The accusations ranged from day-care workers flying around the room, to workers flushing children down toilets into underground tunnels, and even to Chuck Norris being one of the abusers (22).

One form of suggestive technique was "reinforcement." This would include telling the child things like, "Thanks for telling me! You're so smart!" when the child told the interviewer what the interviewer wanted to hear. When the child didn't do that, the interviewer would repeatedly ask, "Are you sure?" To add to this form of reinforcement, the interviewer would say, "Let's see whether you're smart enough to remember what happened!"

It's been noted for some time that reinforcement can strongly shape the behavior of a child, and this was proven time and time again in the McMartin case.

Another suggestive technique that investigators used was "co-witness information." This involved telling the child what other witnesses may or may not have already said. Combining these two suggestive forms would look like this: "Tommy said that you and he got hit by Maria. Tommy is a real smart guy, and I think you could be pretty smart too. Are you going to be a good boy and tell me the same thing that Tommy said?"

This two-pronged approach would reward the child if they repeated what Tommy has said. It combined the fear of being seen as dumb with the fear of being ostracized due to disagreeing with Tommy.

The third suggestive technique was called the "inviting of speculation." This involved telling a child to speculate about what could have happened. An example would be saying, "Becky's butt is bruised. I know you weren't there, but what do you think could have happened?"

This invites the child to make up a story. With the help of positive reinforcement and co-witness information, it solidifies the story in the child's mind.

A fourth suggestive technique required "introducing new information." This is a particularly manipulative technique whereby the interviewer introduces new post-event information (whether accurate or not) into an interview. They do this by asking a question or giving a statement involving information that a child never mentioned; for example, "How often did Maria touch your penis?" But the child had never mentioned his penis.

All four of these techniques led to many preposterous allegations of witchcraft—such as children going through underground tunnels or up in hot air balloons, babies being anally raped with machetes (without physical evidence), and children being flushed down toilets (22).

After the seven-year-long case was finished, all charges were dropped (23). Mind you, the allegations destroyed careers, they left children mentally scarred, and they left the country in a moral panic. In addition, a number of similar cases opened up around the country, where similar false allegations ran rampant. In many of those cases, innocent day-care workers were charged and convicted (24).

Do you know what happened to the CPS investigators in the McMartin case? After they ruined the lives of day-care teachers, brainwashed children into believing absolutely horrific stories, and stirred up a moral panic in the United States? Nothing. Not a single court convicted them of wrongdoing.

In fact, the budget of the National Center on Child Abuse and Neglect went up 1,500 percent. They spent a large portion of that money on the prevention of unproven satanic ritual abuse in the future (25). As usual, the state failed to help individuals, and then it received a raise that was funded by the very individuals it failed to protect.

What Evidence?

Satanic ritual abuse charges aside, suggestive questioning techniques aren't the only issue with CPS's evidence-gathering process. They may base evidence on a story that someone overheard a year ago. For example, "Last year at a barbecue, I heard John say that Martha smokes weed everyday around her kid."

To put this into context, CPS may use evidence based on of a year-old memory (of an accuser), which is based on the story of someone else (John); in other words, on hearsay. In this case, the accuser did not even witness the altercation firsthand, and we don't know whether "John" witnessed it either.

To add to this lackluster evidence-gathering process, the investigator does not write up their report word for word. Instead, his bosses tell him to make small notes, and later create a "narrative" based upon memory of what happened. This narrative can include the environmental settings where the interview took place, the clothing that the interviewee wore, the emotional mood of the person, what the investigator smelled in the house (if the interview is conducted in a home), etc. This doesn't even cover the emotional impact of the questions they ask.

With these notes, the investigator writes a story for the case file. There are several problems with this practice. For one, emotions may deeply affect memory. Small notes written in a hurry can obfuscate what actually occurred. Most importantly, the creation of a story lends itself to adding and removing details. Memory can be tricky, and when investigators rely solely on it in interviews with parents, this inevitably leads to miscalculations and abuse of authority (26). This is why I suggest parents record all interactions with CPS investigators, and I'll go more into this later in the book.

Now, we can demonstrate the issue with this memory-based, evidence-gathering practice through a simple kid's game. It's called the "telephone game" in America.

For people who've never played this game, one person whispers to another person a simple five- to ten-word statement. Others in the room are not supposed to be hear it. They transfer the message about ten times from person to person within the room in under a minute, and then the last person who hears the message repeats it aloud. The last person always hears a completely different (and usually humorous) message compared to the original, and this is when the game is played in under a minute. Now imagine this situation on a larger scale, but instead of ending with an insightful giggle, it leads to the destruction of a family.

Further Issues with Eyewitness Testimony

In a speech given by Stanford Professor of Psychology Barbara Tversksy and Professor of Law George Fisher, entitled "The Problem with Eyewitness Testimony," the two offer great insights into this topic (26):

"Several studies have been conducted on human memory and on subjects' propensity to remember erroneously events and details that did not occur. Elizabeth Loftus performed experiments in the mid-seventies demonstrating the effect of a third party's introducing false facts into memory. Subjects were shown a slide of a car at an intersection with either a yield sign or a stop sign. Experimenters asked participants questions, falsely introducing the term 'stop sign' into the question instead of referring to the yield sign participants had actually seen. Similarly, experimenters falsely substituted the term 'yield sign' in questions directed to participants who had actually seen the stop sign slide. The results indicated that subjects remembered seeing the false image. In the initial part of the experiment, subjects also viewed a slide showing a car accident. Some subjects were later asked how fast the cars were traveling when they 'hit' each other, others were asked how fast the cars were traveling when they "smashed" into each other. Those subjects questioned using the word "smashed" were more likely to report having seen broken glass in the original slide. The introduction of false cues altered participants' memories.

Retelling affects memory, and we rarely tell a story in a neutral fashion. By tailoring our stories to our listeners, our bias distorts the very formation of memory—even without the introduction of misinformation by a third party. The protections of the judicial system against prosecutors and police "assisting" a witness's memory may not sufficiently ensure the accuracy of those memories. Even though prosecutors refrain from "refreshing" witness A's memory by showing her witness B's testimony, the mere act of telling prosecutors what happened may bias and distort the witness's memory. Eyewitness testimony, then, is by definition suspect.

Experiments conducted by Tversky and Elizabeth Marsh corroborate that human memory is vulnerable to bias. In one group of studies, participants were given the "roommate story," a description of incidents involving two fictitious roommates. The incidents were categorized by the researchers as annoying, neutral, or socially "cool." Later, they asked participants to neutrally recount the incidents experienced by one of the roommates, to write a letter of recommendation for a roommate's application to a fraternity or sorority, or to write a letter to the office of student housing requesting the removal of one of the roommates.

When later asked to recount the original story, participants who had written biased letters recalled more of the annoying or "cool" incidents associated with their letters. Participants also included more elaborations consistent with their given bias. They made judgments based upon the annoying or social events they discussed in their letters. Neutral participants made few elaborations, and they made fewer errors in their retelling, such as attributing events to the wrong roommate. The study also showed that participants writing biased letters recalled more biased information for the character they wrote about, whereas they viewed the other roommate neutrally.

In court, lawyers place great import on testimony from an opposition witness who favors their own side's case. For example, defense attorneys focus heavily on prosecution witnesses' recollections of exonerating details. In light of psychological studies demonstrating the effect of bias on memory, the reliance and weight placed on such "admissions" may be appropriate, since witnesses are more apt to tailor their stories—and thus their memories—to the interests of the first listeners. An eyewitness to a crime is more inclined to recount, and thus remember, incriminating details when speaking to police officers intent on solving the crime. If later the eyewitness still remembers details that throw doubt on the culpability of the suspect, such doubts should hold greater weight than the incriminating details.

In another part of the Tversky-Marsh study, they asked participants to play prosecutors presenting a summation to a jury. Participants first read a murder story in which there were two male suspects. Participants were then asked either to prepare a neutral recounting of all they remembered about one suspect, or to prepare a summation to the jury about one suspect. Later, participants were asked to recall the original story. Participants who wrote summations recalled more incriminating details, and wrongly attributed details among suspects more often than participants who originally wrote a neutral recounting."

Those Who Choose to Lie

Sadly, there is more at play in false accusations than just terrible memory. Some people have an incentive to slander others, and I experienced quite a few such cases while I was working for CPS.

For example, in one case a father was accused of working for the Mexican mob, selling cocaine and heroin, running a whorehouse, and being an alcoholic. After a thorough investigation, I found that none of the allegations were true. As it turns out, his neighbor was the accuser. When I asked the neighbor why he came up with all of these false allegations, he stated that he didn't like the guy and knew that there was "something wrong with him." So he decided to make up these absurd allegations to get back at him for "being a dick."

In a case in North Carolina with which I helped after I left the agency, a mother in a divorce case accused a father of sexually molesting his daughter. The mother had actually told the father that she was going to get back at him for being "such an asshole." It took $200,000 for the case to be thrown out. The smoking gun was when the father asked to get a recording of the interview between the caseworker and the alleged victim.

As it turns out, the caseworker used many of the same suggestive tactics used in the satanic ritual abuse cases. The daughter had never directly stated that she was being abused, but simply answered "yes" to a very confusing question that indirectly insinuated sexual abuse. The child had never made any indication outside of this one interview to suggest that she had ever been abused. Even still, after it was proven that the accusation was false and that the investigator had used unethical tactics, the mother was still allowed rights to see her daughter, and no disciplinary actions were taken against the investigator.

In the end, the father was out $200,000, most of his friends no longer saw him because of the accusations, and his daughter was traumatized by the entire incident.

I can recall a number of cases where teenagers would call CPS on other teenagers in order to get back at them for some wrong they had committed. Adults did the same in many poverty-stricken areas, where they used CPS claims as a tool to fight one another. This is partly a result of the fact that people who make false allegations are not convicted for repeatedly doing so. This is why you can have a deranged mother-in-law call CPS on her son-in-law repeatedly because she "just knows" he "smokes the pot." Yet again, it's a matter of incentive. If someone with no ethics can hurt someone else without suffering any consequences, they often do it. CPS is a perfect tool.

There's an emotional and economic cost to these false accusations. They force individuals to call into question valid accusations of abuse, and so undermine legitimate victims. Think of the story "The Boy Who Cried Wolf."

In conjunction with the incentive for false allegations, the outdated and unethical evidence-gathering process, and the terrible training protocol for investigators, there's also the issue of the economic incentives available for the removal of children.

Part 7
Follow the Money

When examining corruption within politics, corporations, or families, it is important to "follow the money." The allocation of money from taxpayers to government agencies has often led to corrupt incentives and mismanagement. This is in part due to a lack of market signals. Without these signals, it is difficult to understand how to best allocate money. As a result, money is often given to agencies that can prove that they are accomplishing their goals.

In the case of CPS, the government takes money from taxpayers and gives it to the agency, under the presupposition that it is going to work to remedy the issue of child abuse. In 1997, the Adoption and Safe Families Act was formally created in order to incentivize CPS and similar agencies to move "abused children" from the custody of their birth parents and into foster homes.

In "The Corrupt Business of Child Protective Services," former congresswoman Nancy Schaefer outlines how this bill led to children being treated as merchandise. The act offered "adoption incentive bonuses" to CPS for every child that the agency removed. Yet again, the "good intentions" of politicians have led to tragic consequences.

There are counties in the United States that offer anywhere from $4,000 to $6,000 to agencies for every child that is removed and placed in a foster home. An extra $2,000 is given in certain cases if the child is developmentally disabled. This money does not go directly into the pockets of workers, but rather is granted to the agency as a whole (27).

As Schaefer outlines:

State Departments of Human Resources (DHR) and affiliates are given a baseline number of expected adoptions based on *population. For every child DHR and CPS can get adopted, there is the bonus of $4,000 or $6,000. But that is only the beginning figure in the formula in which each bonus is multiplied by the percentage that the State has managed to exceed its baseline adoption number. Therefore States and local communities work hard to reach their goals for increased numbers of adoptions for children in foster care . . . [and] there is double dipping.*

The funding continues as long as the child is out of the home. There is funding for foster care, then when a child is placed with a new family, then "adoption bonus funds" are available. When a child is placed in a mental health facility and is on 16 drugs per day, like two children of a constituent of mine, more funds are involved and so is Medicaid; as you can see this program is ordered from the very top and run by Health and Human Resources. This is why victims of CPS get no help from their legislators.

She continues that, due to financial incentives, it is no wonder that very little work is done for reunification between child and parent. The programs that may lead to reunification can be overwhelming and confusing for parents. These programs range from parenting classes, to anger management classes, to counseling referrals, to therapy, etc. All the while, the parent is expected to make a living and keep a nine-to-five job. Then of course, there are attorney fees and thousands of pages of legal paperwork. It can cost families hundreds of thousands of dollars, thousands of hours, and eternal trauma just to attempt to get a child back.

To add to this terrible situation, a vast majority of CPS cases are brought against those who are impoverished. This includes many who cannot even speak Spanish. In these cases, it can become impossible to get a child back due to mistranslations, cost, discrepancies, and mismanagement.

Schaefer continues,

The only way that Child Protective Services stays afloat is by demonstrating that child abuse is rampant—it does not gain more money if it actually eliminates child abuse. So, there's an economic incentive to have as many allegation[s] of abuse to be proven. Now, at CPS we rarely struck out against parents for physical abuse, physical abuse is consider[ed] shaky because spanking kids isn't actually illegal and most parents spank their kids. Instead, CPS uses the war on drugs to get the majority of their convictions. Many of the cases that I dealt with involved the use of marijuana by a parent outside of the home when they were not around their children. In fact, even an admittance of a history of using marijuana even before a child was born is evidence enough for CPS. We could actually do an oral drug test at the home of a father, that father then pass's the drug test, but if the Mother states that they saw the Father smoking cannabis at some point, we could prevent that father from being able to see his child again. CPS was not just supporting the war on illegal drugs, it was profiting off of it and by removing children from their homes and into foster homes, foster homes were then profiting off of the war on children's minds.

Part 8
The Failure of Family Court's Sacred Cow: CASA

Court-Appointed Special Advocates

Before delving into the tragic result of these incentives and foster homes in America, it's important to go into some troubling information regarding Court-Appointed Special Advocates, generally known by the acronym CASA. These advocates are occasionally assigned to cases within family court to be the "child's voice." Now CASA, even amongst advocates against CPS, has become a bit of a sacred cow. It is assumed that they're positive because they don't have the same corrupt incentives as CPS, nor the bureaucracy that leads to the innate problems within any coercive monopoly (28). The trade journal *Youth Today* summed up the appeal of the Court-Appointed Special Advocates program, noting that:

> *[CASA] couldn't sound more apple pie, more thousand points of light. CASAs are a cadre of 74,000 volunteers trained for dozens of hours, then dispatched to conduct independent investigations of child abuse and to represent the children's interests in courts around the nation. What could be wrong with that?*

While helping families who are dealing with family court, I've received reports of mismanagement by the organization and its advocates—CASAs who assume guilt before examination, and who hold a bias toward foster homes, rather than toward family placement. There are well-meaning advocates in the agency, and I've met some of them, but what matters is truth. The fact of the matter is, according to an evaluation commissioned by the National CASA Association, the organization is a bit of a self-admitted failure (29).

The Study

The study facilitated by the National CASA Association found that "CASA's only real accomplishments were to prolong the time children languished in foster care and reduce the chance that the child will be placed with relatives." The study also found "no evidence that having a CASA on the case does anything to improve child safety—so all that extra foster care is for nothing."

A point of contention may be that CASA's main purpose is to handle only "the most difficult cases." The wonderful aspect of this study, which was done by the CASA agency itself, was that the study specifically controlled for this.

The study also found that "when a CASA is assigned to a child who is black, the CASA spends, on average, significantly less time on the case."

Sadly, this is not unexpected to those who have seen how black children are treated within family court and the legal system, in general. The removal of children from homes is heavily tilted toward one particular race—African Americans. According to national data, 37 percent of children in foster care are African American, even though African American children make up only 15 percent of children living in the United States. This carries over to CASA volunteers, who reported spending an average of only 4.3 hours per month on cases involving white children, but only 2.67 hours per month on cases involving black children.

The columnist from *Youth Today* summed up the findings:

The more rigorous evaluation . . . not only challenged the effectiveness of the court volunteers' services, but suggested that they spend little time on cases, particularly those of black children, and are associated with more removals from the home and fewer efforts to reunite children with parents or relatives.

The Elephant in the Room

The issues with CASA may be built into its very structure. The majority of CASA workers see their program as a fun project that will fulfill their want to be "heroes" fighting the "good fight." The majority of them have much different racial and economic backgrounds than their clients. This is a problem seen time and time again within various state agencies. When white people want to "help poor people," you end up with a lot of mistakes.

The white comment isn't a racist throwaway; over 90 percent of CASA volunteers are white and middle class. How could they properly asses a home in a poor neighborhood when they themselves have had a much more privileged background? To a person in the middle class, an entire family sleeping in one bed could come off as negligence. This is not to say that individuals from other demographics can't offer advice, but when that advice is provided through the force of the government, by individuals with very little training, you're going to have some detrimental issues. My own experiences have shown this, as has CASA's study.

One of the most horrifying facts about CASA is that they can be a de facto judge, since the real judge in family court nearly always backs the CASA's recommendations. After the study came out, CASA originally tried to pull it. In the age of the Internet, that's nearly impossible, and it was promptly posted on National Coalition for Child Protection Reform (NCCPR). CASA then began trying to spin the results in their own favor, and thankfully, *Youth Today* showed the truth and categorized CASA's spin as "border(ing) on duplicity."

Assumed Guilt

According to CASA, every evaluation performed by them should be objective—as in, there should not be an assumption of guilt prior to examination. According to the program in Indianapolis—this statement has also been found in other literature devoted to volunteers within the organization—every accused parent is guilty *prior* to examination. According to their own website, "volunteers help ensure that the children we fight to protect are not returned to the very situations where the mistreatment occurred." This statement assumes that mistreatment did occur, which is antithetical to their aim for objectivity (30).

A 'Child's Voice in Court'

Another dubious claim by CASAs is their assertion that they are the "child's voice" in court. This is a very different statement than "in the best interest of the child," which is presumptive in its coercive paternalistic assertion that children—even those who are fifteen years of age—don't have any idea about what is in their best interest. The statement the "child's voice" assumes that the CASAs are stating in court what the child wants, and this is simply not true. CASAs rarely express a child's desperation to go back home, or in rare cases, to stay in a foster home. This further pushes forward one of the most reprehensible aspects of our court system: children, whether seven or sixteen, are assumed to have no idea what they want in life. Obviously, when a child wants nothing to eat but ice cream, we don't give them buckets of ice cream, but that doesn't mean that they should have no say in what happens to them.

Attempt to put this into context: a middle-aged, middle-class white guy with no training in child development, psychology, sociology, or family relations—outside of a couple of hours—is given the authority to voice the wants of a fifteen-year-old African-American girl who was raised in government subsidized housing.

Infantilization is demeaning toward those capable of voicing their own views and asserting their place in the world. Considering that some cases involve teenagers who are capable of conceptualizing right and wrong, it is tantamount to travesty.

Conclusion

Time and time again, when the research is done, we see that family court screws over families repeatedly. CPS and CASA have both been shown to be abject failures, and it's time for them to go. The only way for this to happen is for people to begin to see the truth, and act on it. Whether to confront perpetrators of abuse toward children is a personal, and possibly dangerous, decision. If you witness abuse, don't ignore it. Abusers thrive on secrecy and avoidance of their actions. Let's as a society at least begin in conversation to confront child abuse and its consequences.

Part 9
Foster Homes, Where Good Kids Go to Die

When we try to contemplate the horrendous truth that there are hundreds of thousands of children in America who regularly experience abuse, we begin to seek answers for how to fix the issues. Do we need more education? Do we need to push out more infomercials in the media? Do we need to start just removing kids from their homes?

Though I can empathize with the latter, the government's attempt at this has had catastrophic repercussions. As a result, it is necessary for those who wish to postulate on the positive effects of removal to reorient themselves to the truth. The truth is that the history of foster homes has been a history of abuse.

Current Foster Homes

Before we delve into the grim statistics of foster homes, let's look at why children are being removed from the homes of their families. According to the Foster Care Review Boards' Annual Report of 2004, only 22.4 percent of removals were for physical or sexual abuse. Drug dependency was found to account for 34.2 percent of removals. Judging by similar statistics found in regards to other agencies, marijuana use accounts for a large portion of these (31). This is not to suggest that children who are removed from homes in specific cases are not abused, but that the rubric for what is considered abusive may be too broad. We must keep this in mind when comparing "abusive households" and foster homes.

Abuse in Foster Homes

Let's take a look at how much abuse actually occurs in foster homes. First, there are approximately 400,000 children in out-of-home care in the United States (1). Almost 10 percent of children in foster care have lived there for five or more years. Nearly half of all children in foster care have chronic medical problems. Children in foster care experience high rates of child abuse, emotional deprivation, and physical neglect (10).

A study entitled "Abuse of children in foster and residential care" found that "foster children were 7–8 times, and children in residential care 6 times more likely, to be abused than a child in the general population."

Let me reiterate: Children are seven to eight times more likely to be abused in foster care than are children in the general population (33).

A study of foster children in Oregon and Washington State found that nearly one third reported being abused by a foster parent or another adult in a foster home (34). If we keep in mind that only 22.4 percent of removals are for physical or sexual abuse, it is startling how much actual abuse is occurring in foster homes.

When looking at these statistics, an individual may bring up the fact that correlation and causation are not the same thing; the harmful effects observed in foster homes were simply a result of what the child had experienced before being placed, and not due to the foster homes. A fascinating MIT study worked to separate these variables and came up with some startling facts.

In the study entitled "Child Protection and Child Outcomes: Measuring the Effects of Foster Care," Joseph J. Doyle Jr. found that an abused child placed in foster care is 10 to 20 percent more likely to be arrested, 10 to 20 percent more likely to become pregnant as a teenager, and 10 percent less likely to be working when they become an adult than the abused child who was not placed in foster care (32).

Mental Health and Foster Children

Let's look at the mental health of foster children. In the Casey Family Programs Harvard study, "More than half the study participants reported clinical levels of mental illness after being in a foster home, compared to less than a quarter of the general population"(34).

Post-Traumatic Stress Disorder

Post-traumatic stress disorder, or PTSD—known as "shell shock" during World War I—is a common result of foster homes. For those who have not studied the subject, post-traumatic stress disorder is an anxiety disorder that may develop after a person is exposed to one or more traumatic events, such as sexual assault, serious injury, or the threat of death. The diagnosis may be given when a group of symptoms—such as disturbing recurring flashbacks, avoidance or numbing of memories of the event, and high levels of anxiety—continue for more than a month after the traumatic event.

PTSD causes biochemical changes in the brain and body that differ from other psychiatric disorders, such as major depression. There are detrimental physical issues that occur in the brain—namely alterations in the prefrontal cortex, amygdala, and hippocampus. In some cases, the changes are permanent and come with a slew of side effects.

In one study, 60 percent of children who had experienced sexual abuse in foster homes had PTSD, and 42 percent of those, who had been physically abused while in foster homes, fulfilled the PTSD criteria. The occurrence of PTSD in people who have been abused may not seem rare, but they're not the only ones in these homes who are dealing with it. PTSD was also found in 18 percent of children who were not directly physically abused. These children may have developed PTSD due to witnessing violence in the home (35). I must reiterate that 18 percent of children who were not physically or sexually abused in foster homes had PTSD just from witnessing the abuse of others in the home. Now keep in mind the fact that children are seven to eight times more likely to be abused in foster homes, which means that kids who aren't abused are quite rare.

In a study conducted in Oregon and Washington State, the rate of PTSD in adults who lived in foster care for one year was found to be higher than that of combat veterans. Twenty-five percent of those in the study met the diagnostic criteria—as compared to 12 to 13 percent of Iraq War veterans, 15 percent of Vietnam War veterans, and 4 percent of the general population (34).

The recovery rate for foster home alumni was 28.2 percent, as opposed to 47 percent in the general population (34). Remember that these are just the children who lived in foster care for one year.

Now this is in no way to speak badly about soldiers, but in the modern era—or post draft—troops chose to throw themselves in harm's way. Whether they did so to "fight for freedom" or to "fight for a pay check," they had a choice. Children have no choice whatsoever.

Food Maintenance Syndrome or Bulimia Nervosa

Foster homes are not only affecting child brain development, but also body development. Children in foster care are more likely to suffer from food maintenance syndrome (bulimia nervosa), which is characterized by a set of aberrant eating behaviors. The illness involves "a pattern of excessive eating and food acquisition and maintenance behaviors without concurrent obesity." It resembles "the behavioral correlates of Hyperphagic Short Stature."

This syndrome is hypothesized to be triggered by the stress and maltreatment that foster children are subjected to. The rare disorder is not the only issue, as bulimia nervosa is seven times more prevalent among former foster children than in the general population (36).

Pharmaceutical Drugs and Foster Children

Now we have to get into the discussion regarding pharmaceutical drugs. As has already been explained, there is an incentive to label children "mentally ill" as soon as they enter a foster home. The more mental diagnoses a child has, the more money a foster home receives (27).

A child who's just been placed in a foster home is likely to have issues with temperament, sleeping, and concentration, as they are stripped away from their community, family, school, etc. According to a state mental health practitioner, this means the child has a mental illness, rather than emotional issues that are a result of experiencing a traumatic event. Let's see this in practice.

Studies have revealed that youth who live in foster care, and who are covered by Medicaid insurance, receive psychotropic medication at a rate that is three times higher than that of Medicaid-insured youth who qualify by low family income.

A review that took place from September 2003 to August 2004 examined the medical records of 32,135 Texas children in foster care who were age 0 to 19 years old. It found that 12,189 were prescribed psychotropic medication, meaning an annual prevalence of 38 percent of all the children in these foster homes were prescribed psychotropic medication. The review included children from ages 0 to 2 who are not as likely to receive the drugs. Removing these very young children would undoubtedly reveal a much higher percentage.

A total of 41.3 percent of the 38 percent who received psychotropic medication received three different classes of these drugs in July 2004, while 15.9 percent received four different classes. The most frequently used medications were antidepressants (56.8 percent), attention-deficit/hyperactivity disorder drugs (55.9 percent), and anti-psychotic agents (53.2 percent). The study also showed that youth in foster care are frequently treated with concomitant psychotropic medication—which means two or more psychotropic drugs at the same time—for which sufficient evidence regarding safety and effectiveness is not available (37).

In these cases, a new drug is given to a child to mitigate the side effects of another drug. For example, a child is given Adderall, a stimulant, which then causes them to have issues with temperament and sleeping. Instead of taking the child off the medication, the child is put on a mood stabilizer along with another drug to put them to sleep. The drug interactions in these cases have not been tested in the clinic, so essentially these kids are guinea pigs.

The Economic Expense

The use of expensive, brand-name, patent-protected medication is prevalent in the studies regarding foster children. In the case of SSRIs, the most expensive medications were used 74 percent of the time, as compared to in the general market, where only 28 percent of prescriptions are for brand-name SSRI's instead of generics. The average out-of-pocket expense per prescription was $34.75 for generics and $90.17 for branded products, which shows a $55.42 difference. That's just the economic cost, which I contest isn't as important as the mental and physical effects on the children (38).

The Physical Expense

These drugs come with severe side effects, including increased depression, lower IQ, a lack of brain growth in children, suicidal tendencies, emotional aggravation, anger outbursts—and those are just the mental side effects. Physical side effects can include stunted growth of organs, weight gain for some, and weight loss for others (39).

Homelessness and Foster Children

How do these kids fare after getting out of foster care? Three out of ten homeless people in the United States are former foster children. According to the results of the Casey Family Study of Foster Care Alumni, up to 80 percent do poorly. A third of former foster children are at or below the poverty line, which is three times the national poverty rate. Very frequently, homeless people experienced multiple placements as children. Some live in foster care, but others experienced "unofficial" placements in the homes of family or friends. Here's the real kicker: Nearly half of foster children in the U.S. become homeless when they turn eighteen (36).

Mortality and Foster Children

To finish, let's look at mortality rate. Children are six times more likely to die in foster homes than if they stayed in an abusive household (27).

Conclusion

Let's do a short review of the grim statistics regarding foster children: Foster kids are seven to eight times more likely to be abused than normal children, and nearly half will end up homeless when they age out at eighteen. They are three times more likely to be put on psychotropic drugs, and they are seven times more likely to develop an eating disorder. They are more likely to have PTSD than veterans of war, and less likely to recover from that PTSD. They are more likely to become pregnant as a teenager. They are also 20 percent more likely to be arrested. And tragically, they are six times more likely to die than if they stayed in an abusive family household.

Foster homes are often where kids go to die. It is time to acknowledge that when the state "fixes problems," their policies can result in the blood of the innocent dripping on the floor.

Part 10
Medically Kidnapped

Medically Kidnapped

As I stood in the waiting room of the neonatal intensive-care unit section of the San Antonio Hospital, I knew that in a couple of minutes I would have to deliver information to a mother and it would change not only her life, but also the life of her newborn child. Early on in the mother's pregnancy, during a routine checkup, she tested positive for marijuana. She had smoked weed a couple weeks before she knew she was pregnant, and she admitted this to the doctor. She was again tested in her third trimester, and she tested negative. She said she had smoked pot before she knew she was pregnant, but not after. The baby tested positive for trace amounts of marijuana in his stool sample, however. CPS considers smoking marijuana during pregnancy to be a case of medical neglect, and their rules say they have to take action in order to remedy the issue.

I knocked on the door of the hospital room and the woman let me in. I explained to her—after she had just given birth to a new life—that she would not be able to take the child home, but that the child would be placed in the custody of the state for "safe keeping," and she would have to go to rehab for marijuana. She would have to take classes, interrupt her work schedule, take routine drug tests, and be heavily monitored by the state. If she met all the parameters, went to all the court hearings, and followed everything to the letter, there was a chance she could keep her child.

All of this because she chose to use marijuana and didn't realize she was pregnant. If the mother had chosen to drink alcohol—or use drugs much more dangerous for a pregnant woman and her child (40)—it's very likely that nothing at all would have occurred. Instead, the courts, the child's foster home, the drug testing facility, the hospital, and CPS would all be funded through taxes, with the possibility of pushing this woman to the brink of insanity so that her child would be deemed "safe" according to the state.

After I left the agency, I knew this case was light in comparison to some of the more atrocious ones. Moreover, I had learned that the medical industry's ties to the family court system are—to put it lightly—odious.

What Is Medical Kidnapping?

The term "medically kidnapped" is rather recent, due to what appears to be an epidemic of CPS taking children away from parents after someone has submitted a report when a child goes to the hospital. The reasons for these reports can range from simple misunderstandings by medical practitioners, allegations of parental drug abuse, to legitimate concerns of physical or sexual abuse, and so on. As is the case with most atrocities in life, the intent is usually born from benevolence rather than malevolence.

Primum Non Nocere Means "First, Do No Harm"

The maxim *primum non nocere,* or "first, do no harm," contrary to popular belief, is not a part of the Hippocratic oath that is historically taken by physicians (49). Its moral veracity is far too limiting, but the idea rings true in the minds of most people when interpreting the actions done by doctors. The application of this principle is impossible in the face of government bureaucracy and regulation, and in fact is in opposition to the very nature of government. Government meddling into medicine is not new, and with every tentacle that it wraps around another physician, it hurts more people. The meddling in this context is the extension of the drug war into the relationship between doctor and patient.

Health practitioners, like many other professionals within the United States, are put in a bind when state officials enforce certain guidelines in the event of possible child endangerment (42). As has been outlined in other chapters, child endangerment includes the use of marijuana or other substances that the state defines as "illicit." As a result, the health practitioner is put in the difficult position whereby, even if they don't believe marijuana could hurt a child, the state would consider them criminals if they didn't report the illegal actions of the parent. This creates potentially hostile relationship dynamics between parents and health practitioners, which can make parents afraid to be open with doctors and nurses; as a result, this can endanger their lives and those of their children. The state creates a vicious circle whereby its definition of "the wellbeing of the child" comes before the child's true wellbeing. In actuality, the state is more concerned with the wellbeing of the child protective services and other state and corporate agencies.

Medical kidnapping does not involve a single standalone incident. The concept covers specific actions committed by health practitioners, pharmaceutical companies, and state officials. What follows are multiple examples throughout the last thirty years in which CPS, government welfare agencies, and the medical establishment have colluded in a manner antithetical to the health and wellbeing of children.

The Curious Case of Justina Pelletier

All I want is to be with my family and my friends. . . . It's all I want right now. You're the one who's judging this. Please let me go home, Judge Johnson and Governor Patrick.

Wheelchair-bound Justina Pelletier spoke these words in her YouTube video plea to go home after being held at the age of fifteen against her and her parent's will at the Boston Children's Hospital (43). The following information and timeline are derived from a legal briefing by the Liberty Counsel through correspondence with the medical facilities and victims involved (44).

In the beginning of 2013, Justina—an active figure skater attending a private school in Connecticut—developed flu-like symptoms and received treatment under the direction of Dr. Mark Korson for a rare mitochondrial disease. Dr. Korson is the chief of metabolic services at Tufts Medical Center and a leading expert in mitochondrial disease. Justina began having difficulty eating, and under the advice of Dr. Korson, she visited the emergency room at Boston Children's Hospital (BCH) to see Dr. Alejandro Flores, a gastroenterologist who had treated her before and had recently transferred to BCH. While Justina was at the hospital, a recent medical school graduate and BCH resident named Dr. Jurriaan Peters saw her and adjusted the diagnoses to somatoform disorder.

The new diagnosis dramatically changed the girl's suggested treatment. Somatic symptom disorder (formerly known as a somatoform disorder) is a mental disorder, while mitochondrial disorder (under which she had previously been diagnosed) is biological. In effect, a diagnosis of somatoform disorder says her issues are psychosomatic rather than physical. This means that Dr. Peters believed Justina was subconsciously making herself appear sicker than she actually was.

Diagnoses of this disorder are not without controversy and large risks. Allen Frances, chair of the Diagnostic and Statistical Manual IV task force has stated, "Millions of people could be mislabeled, with the burden falling disproportionately on women, because they are more likely to be casually dismissed as 'catastrophizers' when presenting with physical symptoms" (45).

A physician who wanted to make the claim that a patient is simply making her illness up—after she had already been treated medically by multiple physicians—would need to do so with a preponderance of evidence, which would include gathering such evidence from the previous physicians. Instead, Dr. Peters made the diagnoses without consulting either Dr. Korson or Dr. Flores, whom Justina went to see in the first place.

A psychologist at BCH named Dr. Simona Bujoreanu confirmed the somatoform diagnosis after speaking to Justina for just twenty-five minutes. Dr. Bujoreanu, as it happens, was researching somatoform disorder under a National Institute of Health grant. At the time, in the state of Massachusetts, any ward of the state could be subject to medical research without their consent, even if that research wasn't primarily for the benefit of the ward—in this case, Justina.

BCH requested that Justina's parents sign a new treatment plan. The plan removed all the medications Justina was taking, it prevented her parents from seeking a second opinion, and it placed Justina in a psych ward. It also mandated that the Pelletiers, Justina's parents, never speak to their daughter about her medical treatments or her diagnosis, and never speak to the doctors responsible for her care without prior approval. Essentially, they wanted her to take part in a medical experiment.

The Pelletiers declined, and then worked to discharge their child and return her back to Tufts Medical Center so that she could be seen by Dr. Korson again. Things then went from theoretically catastrophic to criminally catastrophic.

A representative of BCH called CPS, known in Massachusetts as the Department of Children and Families (DCF). The parents were charged with medical abuse and neglect for following the recommendation of specialist Dr. Korson and choosing to refuse a medical experiment treatment plan for their daughter. DCF removed Justina from the custody of her parents and made her a ward of the state. As previously mentioned, in Massachusetts any ward of the state may legally have medical researched performed on them without their consent. *The Boston Globe,* during the course of investigating Justina's story, uncovered at least five other instances of families who have had their children taken by BCH under the same circumstances as the Pelletiers.

BCH kept Justina in a psych ward for sixteen months. They allowed her to see her parents for only one hour per week, as well as make one twenty-minute phone call that was monitored by DCF. The department cancelled numerous visits at the last minute, without any consideration for the parents or the child. They neither permitted nor provided Justina with any form of education or religious services, and her health quickly deteriorated due to a lack of medical treatment and emotional support from her loved ones.

Prior to her incarceration in the psych ward, Justina had been an able-bodied ice skater attending high school. After DCF forced the experimental medical protocol and denied her the medical treatment that Dr. Korson had previously approved, Justina was confined to a wheelchair. Her body strength diminished, she began having indications of sepsis poisoning (inflammation caused by infection) on her abdomen, and her hair began to fall out. By refusing to treat her for her actual medical disorder, and by forcing her into medical experimentation, DCF was killing her.

According to DCF, the condition was in her mind, and her parents were in part to blame. If this were true, however, she would have gotten better as a ward of the state. To make matters worse, the juvenile court imposed an unconstitutional gag order on the parents to prevent them from being allowed to speak to the media about the case. Justina's father, desperate to resolve the issue, decided to go public anyway. DCF sought to hold him in contempt of court. Hundreds of thousands of dollars and a media circus later, a law was named after Justina in order to get her out of state custody and back into the hands of her parents. She was left both physically and mentally crippled, and without an ounce of justice. Unethical medical experimentation like this is not a new phenomenon. In the 1980s and 1990s, states used it heavily in response to the growing HIV/AIDS epidemic.

Pharmaceutical Drug Testing of Orphans

In 2004, the Associated Press (AP) found that government-funded researchers had tested HIV medication on hundreds of foster children in the latter part of the twentieth century (46). The state justified the action by saying that these children were already HIV infected and that, if the state had not turned them into test subjects against their will, the children would not have received any care at all.

The states of Louisiana, Maryland, New York, North Carolina, Colorado, Illinois, and Texas conducted the research. They subjected children—whose ages ranged from infant to late teen—to over four dozen different studies. According to these studies, the children suffered side effects ranging from vomiting to severe rashes, as well as the destruction of their immune systems due to being forced to take antiretroviral drugs. In one study, a researcher stated that they had found a "disturbingly" high death rate among the children who took large doses of the drugs. According to the AP's study, these children had no advocates independent of the foster care or the research agencies. Instead, the states gave money to foster parents and orphanages to conduct untested-drug trials on innocent and unwitting children.

According to Illinois officials involved with the case, none of the near 200 foster children in the Illinois-based AIDS studies used independent monitors, even though the research representatives signed a document that guaranteed "the appointment of an advocate for each individual ward participating in the respective medical research."

Though states have made justifications for testing drugs on unwitting participants "for their own good," the HIV testing was conducted on infant children, meaning that states tested drugs on children who did not need them. Early HIV tests measured CD4 T-cell (white blood cell) counts in order to monitor immune system function. Today, the CD4 T-cell count is no longer considered an adequate HIV test, but during the time of the state-run testing in the 1980s, individuals who had low T-cell counts were considered HIV positive. Now we know that a low CD4 T-cell count may also be associated with viral infections, bacterial infections, malnutrition, psychological stress, and social isolation (47). Children in these orphanages were often

71

victims of physical and emotional neglect and abuse, and this contributed to them having low T-cell counts. The results led to a fair amount of false positive test results and inappropriate and dangerous care.

The Incarnation Children's Center (ICC) in New York City is one of the orphanages where such testing was conducted. According to their published history:

> *Early in the epidemic, HIV disease of childhood was considered to be a down-hill course leading to death. But in the late 1980s, before AZT (an antiretroviral medication) was available, many very ill children admitted to ICC got dramatically better with proper nurturing and high-quality medical and nursing care (48).*

This statement could be interpreted to mean that AZT, rather than AIDS, makes children sick, but a more nuanced interpretation may be that AZT was inappropriately given to children who did not have AIDS in the first place.

Closing Thoughts

It is easy to become disillusioned with the medical establishment in the United States. While researching this chapter, I came across story after story that struck hopelessness within me—a feeling that I believe news agencies aim to create. It was damn near impossible to find concrete examples—with documentation to prove it— of one side acting in a completely malevolent unethical manner against another completely benevolent side. The only party which was always innocent in all proceedings was the children. In a strange way, this could positive. In the real world, there are no saints and no martyrs, and benevolence and malevolence can consequently lie in a null zone. The important part, when trying to find truth, is to remove the veneer of political language. As George Orwell stated, "Political language—and with variations this is true of all political parties, from Conservatives to Anarchists—is designed to make lies sound truthful and murder respectable, and to give an appearance of solidity to pure wind" (49).

Many of the doctors who have made the mistake of working with CPS and other state agencies believed that it was the only option they had. The saddest part is that this is true. The state monopolizes "protection" and prevents grace, tact, and resolution. Doctors are not your enemy any more than a farmer is your enemy—both have a valuable job to do, and both can provide for your wellbeing. The dismantling of the power structures that dictate doctors' actions is the only way to produce a society in which people of good intent can work toward the wellbeing of those who cannot take care of themselves.

Section 2
How to Protect Yourself

The second section of this book is an in-depth analysis of what to do if a Child Protective Services investigator comes to your home. It also contains a thorough analysis of what goes on in CPS courtrooms. It includes what to do and what not do to during any aspect of a CPS case, what to do if you must go to court, interviews with attorneys and judges, as well as answers to the question, "Is Child Protective Services redeemable?"

Part 11
What Can I Do?

You may be wondering what you can do to prevent CPS from coming after you and your family. Every parent is just one phone call away from an investigator knocking on the door. If you are involved in cannabis legalization, homeschooling, or in anything that a person may consider "outside the norm," your chances of someone reporting you to CPS are quite high.

Know What CPS Is

First, you must understand what CPS is. CPS is a disastrous organization that destroys families for economic gain. It's important for not only you, but also for your friends, neighbors, and children to know what this agency is.

How you speak to CPS personnel is up to you. But due to the agency's habit of not letting parents know that their child may be interviewed at school, it is important to tell your child to never—under any circumstances—speak to a CPS investigator alone. CPS investigators are known to fabricate evidence and to manipulate children into making up allegations—whether knowingly or subconsciously.

If you let your friends know about CPS, if you are in a good community among individuals who support you, and your children are aware of how to deal with CPS, you already have a much better chance of dealing with CPS than nearly anyone in the general public. However, there is always a chance for someone to bring a case against you. This is due to the nature of legally required phone calls that hospitals, public schools, and day cares are required to make if they even suspect any kind of abuse.

I've heard of nurses calling CPS because a parent made a joke about marijuana. I've known of teachers calling CPS because a child had a bruise on their leg, and I've known of day-care teachers calling CPS because a parent argued with them. Due to this, knowing what to do if CPS comes after you can be very beneficial.

I have formulated the following suggestions through personal experience, interviews with family court attorneys, and legal advice by family court judges. Not every specific piece of advice will work every time. There is no secret code that will make everything go away. Nevertheless, it is better that you be informed prior to a case than that you try to improvise on the spot. Hundreds of parents have been helped through advice such as that I'm about to share, and this is the first time someone has compiled it all together.

Know Who CPS Investigators Are

CPS is not a stable agency. Investigators don't follow the agency's own rules a good majority of the time, and many of the agents that you may deal with do not know what they're doing or what laws they have to follow. Many of these investigators are lateral bureaucratic movers; they moved from bureaucracy to bureaucracy, wielding power they did not understand, which has results they do not care to acknowledge. They can be dangerous people, and they should be treated as such. They try to catch parents and children off guard in order to get to the "truth." They often use tactics of intimidation, harassment, and manipulation because they believe themselves to be the hero and you to be the enemy.

A CPS Investigator Comes to Your Home

You hear a knock on the door, and someone tells you they're from CPS. They say they are there to talk to you and your child. A trusting person, you open the door. You let the person in, leave them in a room alone with your child, and let them question your child without informing you about anything. Before you know it, you have legal paperwork in your hands stating that CPS is going to remove your child from the home. This is obviously not the correct way to deal with a CPS investigator, but that's what we as a society are taught to do. This is what unknowing parents allow

CPS investigators do. We learn to obey because we have "nothing to hide."

It is important to know your rights. A CPS investigator is not allowed to just barge into your home unless they have a warrant. You're protected by the Fourth Amendment (though often you have to remind legal officials of this, and occasionally they don't care).

Get an Attorney, If You Can Afford One

Understand before you read any of the how-to-guide portion: Get an independent family court attorney, if you can. They are pricy, but they can be unbelievably helpful during this process. If your case goes to court, get your own attorney and tell the court-appointed attorney to hit the road. They are paid case by case, rather than by whether they win. Court-appointed "defense" attorneys have wrecked the lives of many families by convincing them that their case is "unwinnable" and that they should "just do whatever CPS tells them." This is rarely the case with private, family court attorneys, and going to court without one is like taking a knife to a gunfight.

I've seen judges giggle at how people are dressed, and I've overheard investigators discussing how the parent "has no way of winning because they're trying to defend themselves."

Record All Interactions

Before you open the door to a CPS investigator, make sure to have a notepad handy to write everything down—from the date, to the time, to the weather, and everything else. Most importantly, use a recording device.

As stated before, CPS agents' proclivity to undermine the truth in documentation is notorious. The only hope for the facts to come out is if you have the facts on hand. In the age of cheap smart phones and three-dollar tape recorders, it is imperative for individuals to understand the power of keeping people honest by recording everything. If you have a camera, use it as well. The more thorough the recording, the better chance you have to not just share your story, but also protect your rights and demonstrate the truth. It is legal to do so as long as you inform the other party that you will be recording. If they refuse to allow you to record them, then refuse the conversation.

In certain cases, most notably with CPS agencies in New Hampshire (known as the Division for Children, Youth and Families, or DCYF), they may refuse to allow parents to record within the home. Keeping the conversation outside the house allows the recording to occur, so always keep that in mind.

Keep Your Composure

Before CPS, if someone were to come to your home and kidnap your child, you would be justified to do anything in your power to stop the person. Now, so much as raising your voice can signal to the state that you're an unfit parent. It is therefore necessary to keep your cool during any interaction with the agents who approach your door. They will document any misgivings you have toward them as suspicious, threating, and dangerous. Thankfully, with your recording device, you can attempt to keep them honest.

Don't Let the Investigator into Your Home

With the Fourth Amendment in mind, you are now aware that an investigator cannot simply kick their way into your home. Though I've heard of investigators simply walking in without letting anyone know, for the most part they won't just step in, in part due to a fear of litigation or of being shot.

The chances of an investigator having a warrant are slim, as the only way that is possible is if there is enough evidence already against you in order to be able to get the warrant. If an allegation is made through an anonymous tip—which is quite common—then they will not be able to get a warrant at all.

I repeat that you must not let an investigator into your home, even if they state, "I will take your kids, if you don't let me in." This is imperative because investigators can view anything in your home as a death trap.

Legos on the floor equals a filthy floor. Did you forget about cleaning up after the dog? Those are unsanitary conditions. A few dirty dishes equate to horrendous living conditions. Though this may come off as hyperbolic, in a world where CPS receives money for every kid taken, it is not.

If the complaint is that you are a hoarder, you can choose to go into your home and take a few digital photos. Then you can come back to the investigator and show him or her the photos that demonstrate how clean your home is. This can be risky if your house is legitimately cluttered, but it can get the case closed quickly as long as you don't destroy yourself in the interview.

Be Concise, Don't Contradict, and Don't Admit

When you speak with CPS authorities, your goal is to say as little as possible. For someone not acquainted with the agency, the normal reaction to an investigation is to admit to any past wrongdoings. Often parents will divulge every bit of information about themselves and everyone they know. They then assume that the investigator is a good and reasonable person who will see it in their heart that the parent, too, is a great person.

This is not the time to be optimistic. Everything can, and often will, be used against you in a CPS case, and this is important to remember every time you have a yearning to just scream, "But I'm a great parent!"

One of the saddest things about government agents is their manipulation of the most optimistic individuals. This is not to suggest that CPS investigators are all evil sociopaths. But it's important to understand that the training that many of these investigators have gone through tells them to believe that *you* are an evil sociopath.

The truth of the matter is that investigators frequently deal with people who lie to them. They often have come to the point where they are jaded and angry. As a result, they're looking for any discrepancy, any instability, and any story that could trigger them into action, which could lead to a very long and turbulent road ahead for you and your child. Due to this, it is important for parents to refrain from admitting to anything that the investigator could see as abusive.

In the state of Texas, we had a questionnaire that was called a *risk assessment.* The more times we clicked "yes" in answer to its questions, the worse it looked for the parent. For example, "Has the parent ever used marijuana?" Even if you smoked pot in college, this would be used against you.

"Has the parent ever been involved in a domestic violence scenario?" Even if the person who hit you has been out of the house for years, investigators can use the information against you. The list goes on, from your medication history to your history as a child. Admitting as a parent that you were abused as a child is considered a risk factor.

It is your choice to either admit or not admit to these things. The best approach is to try to skirt around the issue. Simply saying, "I don't see how this pertains to the case" can go a long way. If you believe at any time that you are in a situation that is over your head, state categorically, "You can speak with my attorney."

More on that point: If you've had a child removed through the *Termination of Parental Rights,* it's important to get out of your state and don't tell anyone. This is because, under the Adoptions and Safe Families Act of 1997—the same act that caused a large increase in child removals due to financial incentives—CPS now has the right to remove all future children if an allegation of abuse is made. In these cases, the agency will not attempt reunification or reconciliation; instead, they will terminate all existing rights to your children.

In summary: Stay calm, be concise, don't contradict, and don't admit.

Do Not Allow Private Interviews with Your Children

If you don't understand how important it is that you don't allow private interviews with your children, then you haven't been paying attention. CPS investigators will do anything in their power to get a private interview with your child. Do not allow this to happen. You can tell an agent that you're uncomfortable with the idea, and if they insist, you can say that the child has a legal right to have an attorney present during the interview. The investigator will not close the case until they see the child, but that doesn't mean that they can force you to leave them alone with the child.

It is important to tell your child, if they attend public school, that if an investigator comes to their school, the child should say, "I don't want to talk to you without my parents here, and I'm not going to be alone with you."

Your child must understand how important it is not to speak to someone from CPS alone. Children have been removed from their homes, drugged, and physically, mentally, and sexually assaulted when they unknowingly said the "wrong" things to investigators. For the safety of your child, I repeat, say "No" to private interviews with your child.

Don't Sign Anything Unless You Have an Attorney

From medical release forms to safety plans, from termination of rights to acknowledgement of wrongful behavior, the legal documentation that CPS investigators will want you to sign could benefit their side. So many parents have signed statements of admitted guilt, because the investigators stated that nothing would happen and that the case would be closed if they did so. Sadly, the investigators—as they do time and time again—have lied and tricked people into signing these forms. They often do this because a supervisor said that they couldn't leave until the form was signed. Do not sign these forms.

In many states, they have what is called a *safety plan*. This is a voluntary contract—as in, you do not legally have to agree to it. As an investigator, I was told not to let the parent know that. Investigators will attempt to coerce you, but signing it is essentially an admittance of guilt.

These "plans" often contain an agreement to specific rules, which are designed for the "best interest of the child." In certain cases, they will state that "the parent is never to be alone with the child unless a grandparent [or someone else of their choosing] is present." If you are ever accused of "breaking" this plan—such an accusation is considered evidence—then you could have your child immediately removed.

In some cases, the safety plan instructed that the "grandmother must be around the child 24/7." The parent signed without the investigator explaining what the condition actually entailed. This led to confusion on the part of the family, and ended up with a removal due to a lack of their understanding. Confusion is incredibly common—when a family only speaks Spanish, for example. These "safety plans" can create a massive number of rules that can be impossible to decipher and follow. Families are often consciously, or unconsciously, set up to fail.

You may also be asked to sign a "medical release form." This may allow the investigators to view all medical records from your past. If you've ever been diagnosed with mental issues as vague as "depression" or "ADHD," the information can incriminate you. Signing a medical release form can only hurt, not help.

Again, do not sign anything unless you have an independent attorney present.

What Are Collaterals?

In many cases, the investigator will ask the accused parent for names of individuals that the investigator may contact in order to prove or disprove the accusation of abuse. These are known as "collaterals," and they are a double-edged sword. It is a matter of trust between you and the individuals whom you may choose to defend you. It is not necessary to give the CPS investigator names, but it can help with your case.

If you choose to give out this information, make sure that the person doesn't have a criminal background. Also make sure that the person is aware of what CPS is, and tell them to record their conversation with the CPS investigator. Let the person know about the accusation of abuse, advise them on how to answer questions, and let the person know ahead of time that CPS will call them.

I say this is a double-edged sword because many people believe that their friends wouldn't mention anything bad about them. In many cases, I was given the names of collaterals who were actually the very people who accused the parent of the abuse in the first place. The parent gave me the information of a person that they believed would back their story, and that person turned out to be the very one who started the case.

Many people can benefit from the system, and people sometimes assume that abuse is occurring without having any tangible proof. This includes "friends," family members, and friends of friends, who may just come over for a barbecue. So for the sake of your children, be very cautious if you choose to give out the names of potential collaterals.

What to Do If You Know They're Coming to Your Home

You may not know ahead of time that a CPS investigator is coming to your home. If you have advanced preparation, however, this can give you a leg up. Have a notebook to write down what the investigator says. This is called a *case notebook*. Also have an attorney picked out if things are looking bad. Have a recording device as well; video is preferable. And of course, study everything I've written in order to have an understanding of what to expect.

One parent who used the advice presented in one of my presentations told me they managed to get a false CPS accusation thrown out by exposing to the judge that "they (the caseworkers) only have two months of training"; therefore, "How could they make any judgment on what is and what is not abuse?"

She recorded the conversation between the investigator and herself, and demonstrated that the investigator had no idea what the charges of abuse actually were. In just five minutes in court, the case was thrown out. She then contacted Health and Human Services in Washington, DC, and reported that the caseworker was attempting to kidnap her child. After this altercation, the CPS caseworker was not allowed to come back to her home.

There have been numerous parents who have used my advice and have had cases thrown out due to their new knowledge.

What Is a Case Notebook?
Case notebooks can be an integral part of your defense against CPS. Caseworkers keep an organized folder and use a computer program to keep information about you, and it's imperative that you also compile information about the caseworker. This is why a simple binder, folder, or spiral bound notebook can be so incredibly helpful for organization. Here are details that you're going to want to keep in your notebook:

- Write down notes about the accusation and the truth of what actually happened.
- Take notes on all meetings, phone calls, and appointments.
- Record all phone numbers of caseworkers, legal officials, etc.
- Keep visitation notes and foster parent information, if your child has been removed.
- Note down contacts with expert witnesses (medical officials and legal officials).
- Take notes on your daily activities, if the case is going to court.

In regards to the last suggestion: Sometimes the accuser, after the case has already started, claims the parent has been in certain places and in the company of certain people where they should not have been. Though your notebook does not provide solid evidence to back your claim, if a judge asks where you were on a particular day since the case began, having a record of every day will help your case. It also shows the judge that you are prepared, and helps prevent you from making contradictory claims.

For example, John accuses Sarah of being with Bob on August 27, 2014. The case began on June 27, 2014, and it was determined at that time that Bob was a violent abuser. Therefore, Sarah cannot see her child if she spends anytime with Bob. Since Sarah kept notes and had strong collaterals who backed her claim that she was not with Bob on that day, the accusation was thrown out. Though this seems like it may be weak evidence on your side, such evidence has been used and has helped parents in some cases.

An Example Case

You may be wondering how this question-and-answer session could look if you follow my recommendations. Let's do an example.

An investigator comes to a home after someone makes an accusation against a parent that the parent is physically abusing her child. The investigator goes to the child's school, and the child tells the investigator that they are uncomfortable talking to the investigator. This surprises the investigator, who is forced to actually go to the parent's home to talk to the child.

When the investigator arrives there, she knocks on the door. The parent opens up.

"My name is Bianca," says the person at the door, "and I'm an investigator for Child Protective Services. An accusation of abuse has been made that I need to discuss with you. Can I come into your home to discuss this?"

The parent says, "Give me one moment." She grabs her cell phone and clicks record. The parent tells the investigator that she will not participate in the conversation unless she can record it. She explains that it is within her right to record the conversation, and that she is only willing to do the interview if it is done outside. The investigator takes issue with this, but in this case (as in most cases), the investigator allows it, as they don't want to have to come back to the home.

Once they are standing outside, the investigator becomes pushy and begins asking questions. Before the parent answers anything, she asks the investigator for details about the accusation. The investigator might push back on this, but the parent remains firm that she is within her rights to know what she has been accused of before answering any questions. The investigator explains that the accusation is in regards to physical abuse. The parent tells the investigator that she has never physically abused their child. The investigator then says that she has some questions.

"What is your full name, what is your phone number, what is your social security number, what is your birth date, and what is your address?" At this point, there's nothing wrong with giving out the majority of this information, as they most likely already have it. Whether you give out your social security number is obviously up to you.

"Who is living in the home?" This question can hurt you. If it's simply you living in the home with the other parent and your child, then I'd simply answer the question. If there are ten people living in the home, and this is not readily apparent to the investigator—i.e., the only car outside is your own—I would simply state that the question has nothing to do with the case.

Otherwise, everyone in the house could end up being questioned. If you're living with a large number of people, they are just more people whom CPS will want to question and who could hurt your case. If anyone in the home has a criminal background, your child could then be removed. If just one individual in the home has as much as a theft charge, the power is then placed in the hands of the investigator, and this could put you and your family in danger. This is why it's important for your child not to talk to the investigator. By choosing not to answer, rather than choosing to lie, you won't incriminate yourself.

"Have you ever had a CPS case in the past?" If you have not, obviously you can answer "no." If you have had a CPS case in another state, you can choose to answer "no." Getting records from other states is incredibly difficult and is rarely done. If you had another CPS case in the same state, you can choose not to answer—especially if you lost the case—or you can answer "yes" and explain the case, if it was ruled in your favor.

"Have you ever used drugs in the past?" asks the investigator. Reply "no," or if you have been tried and convicted for drug possession, simply do not answer. In either instance, let the investigator know categorically that this has nothing to do with the CPS case.

"Have you ever been a victim or perpetrator of domestic violence?" State "no," or if you have been tried and convicted for domestic violence, simply do not answer. In either instance, state categorically that this has nothing to do with the case.

"Do you have a criminal background?" If you have been found guilty of a crime in another state, you may choose to state "no." As with past CPS cases, getting records from other states is difficult for the investigator and is rarely done. If you have been convicted in the state that you're in, do not answer, and instead say that the question has nothing to do with the case. If you have never been convicted or charged with anything, obviously reply "no."

"What was your childhood like?" This question is set up to hurt you. Simply do not answer. Tell the investigator that this doesn't pertain to your case, and then move on.

"How do you discipline your child?" Though spanking is legal in all states in the U.S., admitting to it can get you in trouble quickly. Say that you speak to your child about what they did wrong, that you use "timeout," if you do, and that your child rarely breaks any rules. All of these points look good in regards to your case. It shows that you're capable of positive communication, that you're a soft disciplinarian, and that you're capable of raising a "well-behaved" child.

I do not justify spanking, and I would recommend anyone interested in other means of discipline read the book *Parent Effectiveness Training: The Proven Program for Raising Responsible Children*, by Thomas Gordon. That said, a child raised in a home where parents use light spanking seems to be better off than one raised in a foster home, according to statistics.

If the investigator hasn't already seen your child, they are going to want to talk to them. This is where things can go wrong or right. If your child has any bruising from something outside of actual physical abuse—falling off a bike, fighting with friends, or any of the million other ways that kids can hurt themselves—the investigator could possibly charge you with physical abuse. If you can help it, I wouldn't allow the investigator to see the child until after you go to a trusted doctor. They can provide you with documentation proving your claim that the bruise came from a fall, or something along those lines. If your child has no bruising, then bringing the child outside to see the investigator so that the person can witness that the child is fine and fed can help move your case along.

If your child is under the age of thirteen, I would suggest that you don't allow an interview at all. Investigators can manipulate kids, even in front of the parent. If your child is of a mature age and is aware of what to do and what not to do when talking to an investigator, it's best to be in the room with the child while the interviewing process is going on. As has already been said, *never allow private interviews with your child.*

Part 12
Preparing for Court

If your case goes to court for external reasons, you need to be prepared. I always recommend that you have your lawyer with you. In the case of a removal, you will be notified in writing and you will receive a copy of the documents that were filed with the family court.

One of the documents is called a *petition*, which is written after a report is received and investigated by CPS. The "respondent" in the petition is the parent who allegedly committed the abuse. The petition will list the allegation or allegations (which will be located within the affidavit attached to the petition given to the parent). There will be a statement of the charges that CPS alleges to have occurred, and the reasons why your child needs to be removed and placed into the hands of the state. It's important to know your rights (51).

Know Your Rights

You have the right to an attorney. If you cannot afford to pay for an attorney, and CPS is seeking to terminate your parental rights, you may ask the judge to appoint an attorney for you. I recommend that you do not take one of these court-appointed attorneys.

You have the right to admit or deny the allegations made about you and your family.

You have the right to be notified of all court hearings.

You have the right to attend all court hearings and meetings.

You have the right to an interpreter in court if you do not understand English, or you are hearing impaired.

You have the right to talk to your CPS caseworker and your attorney.

Though these are your rights, CPS has created many obstacles to interpretation. In some cases, the obstacles may come as a result of the investigator holding a grudge against you, but in most cases it is due to mere incompetence. It is up to you to be competent. Be aware of your rights, for they are a weapon that you can use to benefit you in your court case.

Who Will Be Present in Court

CPS Caseworker

Obviously, the CPS caseworker will be involved in the case, and as they called for a removal, you can assume which position they hold regarding the allegation. If the case leads to what is known as a *service plan* (this will be explained further later on), the caseworker will "work with you" to accomplish the necessary conditions.

Your Attorney

Don't accept court-appointed attorneys. Judges, CPS investigators, courts, and court-appointed attorneys are all employed by the same people. Court-appointed attorneys are easy to walk all over, rarely contest cases, and in many instances, simply tell you to admit to wrongdoing.

Choose a private family court attorney. Not every attorney understands family law, but many will act as if they do in order to collect a profit. Listings for family court attorneys by state are available online.

It's important to give your attorney all the information regarding the case, as good representation is only possible when they know what they're representing. Your attorney will talk with you before every hearing, and speak for you in court (in most cases). They will also help you understand your rights, tell you about the hearings you will attend, and tell you what to expect at each hearing.

The Attorney for CPS

CPS has an attorney, as well, who helps "prove" the allegations of abuse.

The Child's Attorney, or the Attorney Ad Litem

Your child will have an attorney representing them in the case. This person is referred to as the Attorney Ad Litem (AAL), and they are appointed by the court. The Attorney Ad Litem's job is to meet with your child and act as an advocate on behalf of the child. They also serve as the Guardian Ad Litem (GAL) for the child in certain cases. The Attorney Ad Litem is in many cases a mouth piece for CPS, and is not to be trusted.

The Court-Appointed Special Advocate (CASA)

Even with the self-admitted failure, the agency is still booming. Within court, the CASA representative reports on how the child is doing and what the representative feels is in the child's "best interest." Sometimes the child advocate may also be called a Guardian Ad Litem (GAL).

Part 13
When Will You Have to Go to Court?

If your child is removed, then you may be asked to attend several court hearings and other meetings. These are set up so that the judge and others involved can listen to the parents, caseworkers, and everyone else. From there, the court can decide what will "help your family." Most child abuse and neglect cases have at least eight different court hearings and meetings during the first year:

- Emergency hearing
- Adversary hearing (show cause hearing) or mediation
- Initial permanency planning team meeting (PPT)
- Status hearing
- Initial permanency hearing
- Additional PPT meetings
- Permanency hearing
- Final hearing (the trial)

It is integral to winning your case and protecting your child that you appear at every hearing on time. The hearing will start whether or not you're there. This is why keeping everything organized in your case notebook is vital to winning your case, and you don't want to lose everything because you thought a case was at 1:00 p.m. rather than at noon. Each hearing has its own purpose, and for the sake of being thorough, I'll explain every one of them. The timetables presented show the family court system protocols in Texas, and can vary depending on the state (40).

Emergency Hearing

If a child is removed from their home without a court order, an emergency hearing will be held within one business day of when the petition is filed in the family court. This may take place without the parent there. This hearing occasionally occurs over the phone. At the hearing, the judge is given whatever incriminating information the caseworker has to justify the removal. The judge decides whether temporary custody by CPS is necessary from that time until the adversary hearing. This is one of the more frightening times of the case. Often, the parent has had no say in the scenario beforehand, and the future of their child is in the hands of strangers.

Adversary Hearing (Show Cause Hearing)

Generally, the adversary hearing is held before the fourteenth day after the initial removal of the child. The function of the hearing is to determine whether the emergency removal was necessary. CPS can also get temporary orders during the hearing to keep the child away from their caregiver until the case is over.

This hearing is crucial for you, as the parent, and can turn into a make-or-break scenario meant to ensure the safety of your child. You will need to make your case and explain how you can go about protecting your child in the future. I will outline what to do and what to say during the hearing later in the book.

Permanency Planning Team Meetings

The permanency planning team meeting is generally held between 30 and 45 days after the removal of the child from the home, and occurs again, if necessary, in the fifth, ninth, and thirteenth months. This isn't technically a court hearing, as there is no judge present. Stating this, the attorneys, the children (if over twelve years old), the foster parents, as well as the accused, the CPS staff members, and any other caretakers may be there. If the accused parent has an attorney, it may be beneficial to have them at these meetings in order to prevent bullying, manipulation, and other corrupt actions committed in CPS cases. The parent can also bring family members, if the family members bring benefit to the case.

At the first permanency planning team meeting, a "service plan" is created. The plan will include goals for the child, such as:

- Reunification with parent(s);
- Termination of parents' rights to the child;
- Placement of child with relatives;
- Placement of child in foster care; or
- Adoptive placement

Requirements of this service plan—whether they be parenting classes, anger management classes, drug rehabilitation, etc.— must be achievable. If you work regular day hours and the service plan requires you to complete classes during the day, you must plead your case to ensure success in these requirements. If you are unable to fulfill the requirements, this can destroy any chance for reunification between you and your child.

Status Hearing

At the status hearing, the parent and their attorney appear before a judge to discuss the newly created service plan. This hearing is generally held within 60 days of when the child was taken by CPS. At the status hearing, a discussion of the service plan occurs, along with orders by the judge that ensure that the parent knows that this plan must be followed, or they risk losing their child forever. Coercion and manipulation are to be expected here, as per usual, which is why an attorney can be integral in the case.

Permanency Hearing

The initial permanency hearing must be held no later than 180 days after CPS takes hold of the child. Within this hearing, an evaluation of the permanency plan for the child is performed by the judge. The judge reviews the case, checks that the parent is fulfilling the requirements within the service plan, and makes changes in the plan at this time, if necessary. If an agreement on the changes is made between CPS, the parents, and the judge, then the service plan can be changed.

The judge will check to see whether the parent has made changes that will lead to the safety of the child. If the judge finds these changes to be adequate, the child can be returned to the parent, with restrictions. The judge can also decide that the child will remain in state care, if he or she doesn't believe the child will be secure with the parent.

At the end of the hearing, the judge can set a date for dismissal, as well as give notice in open court of that date to all parties, the day of the next permanency hearing, and the trial date.

Final Hearing (the Trial)

The court must make a final order before the first Monday after the first anniversary of the original order that appointed CPS temporary managing conservator, unless the court granted an extension of no more than 180 days on or before that date.

A final order can be one that:

- Requires that the child be returned to the parents;
- Names a relative of the child, or another person, to be the child's managing conservator;
- Without terminating the parent-child relationship, appoints CPS as the managing conservator of the child;
- Terminates the parent-child relationship and appoints a relative of the child, another suitable person, or CPS as the managing conservator.

For all final hearings, testimony and evidence regarding the "best interest of the child" will be offered by everyone involved.

Part 14
Your Day in Court

Dress the Part

In all your meetings and hearings, it is important to look the part of a respectable citizen. Dress well. I can recall more than a few cases where parents appeared in court dressed in T-shirts—one mother wore a shirt saying "f*ck you"—and as a result they were immediately not taken seriously.

When you go to court, it's not the time to give the finger to the fashion industry. You're there to save your child, not to show off your favorite band or funny quote. Numerous studies demonstrate that people who are dressed in professional clothing are respected more than those who dress in sportswear such as Sean John clothing. This isn't very complicated. You can find a suit and tie for $10 at any thrift store. Dressing the part gets you that much closer to winning your case. Take a shower, dress well, and don't show up drunk.

What to Take with You

The case notebook is essential to helping with your case. At every meeting, during every discussion regarding your case, at every hearing, and any time that you are dealing with your case, it is important to keep everything in your case notebook and have it with you at all times. Refer to the section entitled "What is a Case Notebook" for a thorough example of what should be in the notebook.

Get Your Story Straight

This is one of the most important aspects of your case. If you have your notebook, which backs your story, you're already way ahead of most parents. The important thing is to keep your case notebook organized, along with all your evidence for your rationale that explains why your case should be thrown out. Most importantly, don't contradict yourself, and don't provide evidence that will incriminate you.

As already mentioned, some types of information that can incriminate you are the admittance of prior drug use, domestic violence, your childhood history of being abused, political affiliation, and so on. As has been stated previously—be concise, don't contradict, and don't admit. Speak firmly. Your words can ensure or destroy your future with your child.

Know Your CPS Caseworker

This book has exposed many of the horrific aspects of CPS and family court. In all of your meetings and court hearings, expect negligence, manipulation, coercion, threats, incompetence, and stupidity from many of the people you will be dealing with. It's important, in the face of pure absurdity, to keep your composure, stay organized, know your rights, and try your best not to emotionally break down in front of these people.

In an interview, Attorney Seth Hipple described most CPS caseworkers as "ill prepared bureaucrats" who rarely know the restrictions, regulations, and procedures found in their own handbooks. Rarely does anyone actually know what the protocol is for speaking while there's a recording device in the room, the legality of specific removals, the limitations of power, or any aspect of parental rights.

The caseworker, though, is not your main audience within court cases. That position belongs to the judge in your court hearing.

Part 15
Dealing with Judges in Court

What follows are recommendations that were presented at the Association of Family and Conciliation Court Conference in 2011. A workshop was held called "Dealing with Difficult Judges" presented by Judge Carole Curtis and Judge Roselyn Zisman. Thanks to Thurman Arnold for summarizing much of the workshop (50).

By the time you arrive in court, the power has shifted from the caseworker to the judge. It is always important while in court to remember that you're pleading your case to the judge, and not to CPS or their attorneys. If you want a surefire way to make nearly any judge angry, start arguing using legalese. If you and or your attorney want to bring other people into the courtroom, let the court know all of this beforehand as well. Uncontrollable people lead to uncontrollable and subjective rulings by judges.

Finding Out Information

It can be helpful to find out about the judge in your particular case. In many jurisdictions with direct calendar assignments, you can find out which judge will be there for your particular case. Any good family attorney in your area should have some information on every judge in the jurisdiction. Some judges actually side with families more often than others, and obviously this can be a benefit to your case. Attorneys who know which way a particular judge rules—if the judge is predictable—will be able to give you tips on how to handle them. This is just another reason why it is so important to have an attorney with you in court.

You can also get a leg up in court by actually observing family court judges before your court hearing. In many counties, family court cases are open to the public. You can learn valuable information about the way in which a specific judge acts by watching cases yourself. Does the judge reprimand parents who raise their voice? Are they the type of judge who listens intently, or one who looks like they're daydreaming during hearings? Of course, this isn't a 100-percent certain way to learn everything about how a judge will act on your day in court. Hell, if the judge is hungry and tired, he might just be extra forceful on your court day, and you'll fight an even more uphill battle. Subjectivity is an enemy to the truth, but knowing the person can help you win over their subjective preference.

Don't Assume That the Judge Has Read Your Case File

Recognize that the judge most likely only knows CPS's side of the argument, and you will have to plead your case in a respectful and non-confrontational manner. Do not assume that the judge has read the case file, but also don't bring the fact up in court.

In legal testimony, your best bet is to assume that the judge has not read the case file or the history for your case. If they have read it, they will most likely let you know. You should present your information in an orderly fashion, with highlights and sound bites. Make sure to leave out the non-important details that confuse the case and can lead to contradictions. Having an outline in advance is always helpful. Practicing before the case is beneficial, so that even when emotions are high, you and your attorney are prepared.

Damage Control

If the judge begins to butt heads with either you or your attorney, it is your role to deal with "damage control." Lowering the tone of your voice and switching from emotional terminology to legal terminology is helpful. Also, slow and respectful speech patterns can help in defusing the situation before the case goes to hell. As Judges Curtis and Zisman put it, "You must do whatever you can to end this contest. Consider a retreat, whatever that means in the circumstances. Move your reaction into this range . . . : be calm, be measured, be focused, and be polite (be unfailingly polite)."

Judge Curtis and Zisman both note, "Some judges are rude, aggressive, even abusive, for no apparent reason, or at least none that justifies this behavior. It is extremely important for the lawyer (or the party) to be calm, and to remain calm, polite, [and] focused."

The majority of these types of judges are on a power trip, and in order to deal with that issue, it's important not to undermine them. Eloquence and brevity are your friend, as well as confidence and due diligence in your testimony. Treating the judge as though he is your enemy within court will get you nowhere. I'm not suggesting that he is your friend, but in a world where one man has the power to make or break your family, it is important to get him on your side. A large portion of your court case can end up involving damage control, and it's important not to be brought down by the negativity of judges or attorneys when you are on the side of right.

Part 16
Court Hearing Procedures

In most family court hearings, a judicial assistant will call you and your attorney into the courtroom and tell you where to sit. As soon as you get to your seat, prepare your paperwork and documents before the hearing starts. Next, the judge will walk in, and you will be told to "rise" (stand). Then you'll be told to sit. This is obviously a way for the judge to demonstrate his power. In the majority of cases, the attorney with the CPS investigator will make an opening statement. The judge may ask the investigator and/or the CPS investigator's supervisor a series of questions in regards to the case. No matter what is stated, no matter what fabrication or manipulation, do not begin interrupting the investigator or the attorney. This seems obvious, but when emotions get flared, it is easy to lose your composure.

Next, you and/or your attorney will offer evidence to support your ability to ensure the safety of your child. A back and forth may occur, and depending on the type of hearing (look at the specific case types in the previous chapter) the judge may make a decision and write it in a court order. Let's look at an average court proceeding.

A Normal Court Proceeding

1. The Person who filed the petition ("petitioner") or motion ("movant") that resulted in the hearing makes an opening statement, or the judicial officer may ask questions.
2. The other side(s) ["respondent(s)"] makes his/her/their opening statements.
3. Petitioner/movant tells his/her side of the story first. This can be the Attorney Ad Litem, the Guardian Ad Litem, the CPS caseworker's supervisor, and/or the CPS caseworker.
4. Respondent (accused) and/or respondent's attorney pleads their

case.

5. Petitioner/movant makes a closing argument. (This doesn't always occur.)

6. Respondent (accused) makes their closing argument. (This doesn't always occur.)

7. Judge, commissioner, or special master makes a decision and writes it in a court order.

Telling Your Side of the Story

Much has been discussed in this book regarding what to state and what not to state in any case regarding CPS. The same is true in court hearings. It is important to understand that standing up and yelling out "the truth" will not simply make everything go away. I am amazed at how often people assume that court is similar to what they see on television.

If you follow the legal suggestions given, court will be a lot more understandable. It may not allow you to "win" the whole case—there is no winning in family court—but at least it will help ensure the future safety of you and your family. Within court, there are instances in which you can have your attorney speak for you entirely, but where this does not occur, the following describes what speaking for yourself will look like.

Telling Your Side in Court

1. You are "sworn in" or you "affirm."

2. You tell the court the information you want the court to know. This is called "direct examination." Make sure to review the "dealing with judges in court" section of this book.

3. The other side may then begin asking you questions. This is known as "cross examination." Keep your composure, don't contradict, stay brief, be organized, and be nimble.

4. You may then provide more information regarding your case, if the court allows it. This is known as "re-direct examination."

5. A "re-cross examination" may occur where the other side may ask more information.

6. The court will then tell you to return to your seat.

Additional Information

Are There Any Other People at the Hearing Who You'd Like to Provide Additional Information to the Court?

If you choose to have someone else help plead your case, it is imperative that they are just as prepared as you are. All of the above information for court preparation should be gone over with your witness, and practicing with them prior to the case, if possible, is recommended. If you choose to do this, here is the general process that occurs:

1. The person ("witness") are "sworn in."
2. You or your attorney ask the person questions that will help your case ("direct examination").
3. The opposing side, or the judge, may choose to ask the person questions about their statements ("cross examination").
4. If the court allows it, you may then ask more questions, but only in regards to the the opposing side's questions or statements ("re-direct examination").
5. The judge may ask the witness additional questions, and then tell the person to either leave or stay at the court proceeding.
6. If another witness joins in, the process is started again.

Closing Statements Regarding Court Advice and Information

The court case examples given are not the same, and should not be assumed to be the same, in every state or jurisdiction. Different states have different procedures, and I chose to outline a general idea of what most court hearing processes are like. Of course, an attorney can advise you on the ins and outs of your particular case, and online resources may also be helpful for preparation. My suggestions for court should not be thought of as a 100 percent guaranteed way in which to protect yourself, but they do give you a CPS insider's perspective on court, along with information from judges and attorneys, on dealing with specific circumstances.

For more information regarding legal documentations and resources, go to legallykidnapped.net.

Part 17
Closing Thoughts

Since dispelling the truth about CPS a little over a year ago—first on my podcast *Truth Over Comfort,* and then in public speeches and television interviews—a number of parents, advocates, and pundits have wanted my thoughts on how to reform the system for the better. I must admit that I don't know whether reform is possible.

The problem is that the system does in fact benefit those who work in it, and the way that it becomes better for them is to clamp down and destroy more lives while milking those lives for more cash. The system was not set up to help those outside of the system, for state-controlled agencies exist outside of the ethical mechanisms of exchange; rather, they are parasitical in nature.

The state does not create wealth, but rather leaches off the work of the productive until there is nothing left to take. The money state workers make in the family court system is a redistribution of wealth through the threat of adult kidnapping—prison—in order to pay others to kidnap children from their parents. To simplify, *the state steals money—taxes—from parents in order to use that money to kidnap children from those very parents.* This is why reform may be impossible, for the very nature of the system is unethical and based on the destruction of others.

A bit of hopelessness may come from this acknowledgement, but I see it as a form of mental empowerment: *if we devote our lives to that which is outside of our control, we inevitably suffer.* To battle that over which we have no power—while ignoring the power we do have—is to waste both our time and our lives.

I teach people how to tame and move around the leviathan—otherwise known as the family court system, and its soldiers known as CPS investigators—and I fight for the rights of children by suggesting peaceful means of fostering their ability to thrive in this world—peaceful parenting. Our ethics, values, integrity, and discipline are within our sphere of control; begging politicians who have none of these traits to change is like hitting your head against the wall for eternity while watching this short life go by without you. I am not shaming those who work against the state, through state mechanisms, but simply offering a different way to go about change. Take control of your own life, protect and love your children in the best way you can, and attempt to find freedom through your relationships with the people in your own life.

I will help people fight the courts if that time comes, but we first need to learn prevention through practice, and peace through making good choices. Teach others in your community that calling state workers is antithetical to the safety of children, and empower individuals to take matters into their own hands through understanding first, confrontation second, and community pressure third. This will do more to fight the system, for to undermine the system is to kill it. This is within your control. This is how you acknowledge that *you are not a slave to any man, woman, or government.*

I thank you for reading this book. You can find further information regarding the nature of the state, the nature of child protective services, and on how to challenge the system at cpsvictimsupport.com.

References

Introduction
1. U.S. Department of Health and Human Services, Administration on Children, Youth and Families. The AFCARS Report: Preliminary FY 2006 estimates as of January 2008. Washington, DC: U.S. Government Printing Office; 2008
2. Zerbe, Richard O., Robert D. Plotnick, Ronald C. Kessler, Peter J. Pecora, Eva Hiripi, Kirk O'Brien, Jason Williams, Diana English, and James White. "Benefits And Costs Of Intensive Foster Care Services: The Casey Family Programs Compared To State Services." *Contemporary Economic Policy*: 308–20.

What Is Child Protective Services?
3. "Child Protective Services: A Guide for Caseworkers. 2003." Child Protective Services: A Guide for Caseworkers. January 1, 2003. Accessed September 21, 2014.
4. Wang, Kechin. "The Continuing Turbulence Surrounding the Parens Patriae Concept in American Juvenile Courts." McGill Law Journal. Accessed September 21, 2014.
5. Early, Barbara, and Michele Hawkins. "Opportunity and Risks in Emerging Family Policy: An Analysis of Family Preservation Legislation." *Children and Youth Services Review* 16, no. 5–6 (1994): 309–18.
6. Mehler, Barry. "Brief History of European and American Eugenics Movements." 1988.
7. Black, Edwin. War Against the Weak: Eugenics and America's Campaign to Create a Master Race. New York: Four Walls Eight Windows, 2003.
8. Helms, Ann, and Tommy Tomlinson. "Wallace Kuralt's Era of Sterilization." Charlotte News Panthers Hornets Sports Banking. September 26, 2011. Accessed September 21, 2014.
9. Indian Child Welfare Act, (Pub.L. 95–608, 92 Stat. 3069, enacted November 8, 1978, 25 U.S.C. §§ 1901–1963).

10. Barbell, Kathy, and Madelyn Freundlich. "Foster Care Today." Casey Family Programs National Center for Resource Family Support, 2001.

A Culture of Fear
11. Brzezinski, Zbigniew. "Terrorized by 'War on Terror.'" Washington Post. March 25, 2007. Accessed September 21, 2014.
12. Skenazy, Lenore. "Poll: Most Americans Want to Criminalize Pre-Teens Playing Unsupervised." Reason.com. August 20, 2014. Accessed September 21, 2014.
13. "TITLE XVIIIFISH AND GAME." CHAPTER 207 GENERAL PROVISIONS AS TO FISH AND GAME. July 1, 2001. Accessed September 21, 2014.
14. "State v. Whiteley, 172 NC App 772 (04–636) 08/16/2005." State v. Whiteley, 172 NC App 772 (04–636) 08/16/2005.
15. Bonner, Ryan. "Police: Mom Leaves Son in Lego Store While She Shops at Mall." Patch. August 6, 2014. Accessed September 21, 2014.
16. McCann, Kate. "Police: Woman Arrested for Leaving Child inside Car at Whole Foods—Southtown Star." September 3, 2014. Accessed September 21, 2014.
17. Glassner, Barry. The Culture of Fear: Why Americans Are Afraid of the Wrong Things. New York, NY: Basic Books, 1999.

How the Case Starts
18. Skenazy, Lenore. "A Dad Lets His Kids Play Outside—and Child Protective Services Comes Calling." The Agitator. August 3, 2013. Accessed September 21, 2014.
19. "Texas Family Battles Judge over Homeschooling." WND. January 1, 2014. Accessed September 21, 2014.
20. Breathes, William. "Colorado Drug-Endangered Child Bills Threaten Legal Marijuana-Using Colorado Parents." April 9, 2014.

Satanic Ritual Abuse
21. Spanos, NP: Multiple Identities & False Memories: A Sociocognitive Perspective. American Psychological Association. pp. 269–285 1996.
22. Schreiber, Nadja, Lisa D. Bellah, Yolanda Martinez, Kristin A.

Mclaurin, Renata Strok, Sena Garven, and James M. Wood. "Suggestive Interviewing in the McMartin Preschool and Kelly Michaels Daycare Abuse Cases: A Case Study." *Social Influence*: 16–47.

23. Reinhold, Robert. "The Longest Trial—A Post-Mortem; Collapse of Child-Abuse Case: So Much Agony for So Little." The New York Times. January 23, 1990. Accessed September 21, 2014.

24. DeYoung, Mary. "Two Decades after McMartin: A Follow-Up of 22 Convicted Day Care Employees." *Journal of Sociology & Social Welfare* 34, no. 4 (2007). December 1, 2007.

25. Waterman, Jill. Behind the Playground Walls: Sexual Abuse in Preschools. New York: Guilford Press, 1993.

What Evidence?
26. Engelhardt, Laura. "The Problem with Eyewitness Testimony." Stanford Journal of Legal Studies: A Talk by Barbara Tversky and George Fisher.

Follow the Money
27. Shaefer, Nancy. "The Corrupt Business of Child Protective Services." Georgia State Senate, 50th District. September 25, 2008.

The Failure of Family Court's Sacred Cow: CASA
28. Barbara White Stack, "An Evaluation of Volunteers Courts Controversy," Youth Today, July 2004.

29. Caliber Associates, Evaluation of CASA Representation: Final Report (Undated, but published in 2004).

30. Karen Pittman, "Evaluation: Risk or Responsibility," Youth Today, October, 2004.

Foster Homes, Where Good Kids Go to Die
31. Wheeler, Melinda, Patrick Yewell, and Kevin Smalley. "Citizen Foster Care Review Board 2004 Annual Report." Kentucky Court of Justice. January 1, 2004.

32. Doyle, Joseph J. "Child Protection and Child Outcomes: Measuring the Effects of Foster Care." American Economic Review: 583–610.

33. Hobbs, GF; Hobbs, CJ; Wynne, JM (1999). "Abuse of children in foster and residential care." Child Abuse & Neglect 23 (12): 1239–52.

34. Casey Family Programs, Harvard Medical School (2005.04.05).

"Former Foster Children in Oregon and Washington Suffer Posttraumatic Stress Disorder at Twice the Rate of U.S War Veterans."
35. Dubner, AE; Motta, RW (1999). "Sexually and physically abused foster care children and post-traumatic stress disorder." Journal of Consulting and Clinical Psychology.
36. Schofield, Gillian. "What Works in Foster Care? Key Components of Success from the Northwest Foster Care Alumni Study Peter Pecora, Ronald C. Kessler, Jason Williams, A. Chris Downs, Diana J. English, James White and Kirk O'Brien Oxford University Press, New York, 2010, Pp. v." Child & Family Social Work: 375–76.
37. Zito, JM; Safer, DJ; Sai, D; Gardner, JF; Thomas, D; Coombes, P; Dubowski, M; Mendez-Lewis, M (2008). "Psychotropic medication patterns among youth in foster care." Pediatrics 121 (1): e157–63.
38. Cascade, EF; Kalali, AH (2008). "Generic Penetration of the SSRI Market." Psychiatry (Edgmont (Pa.: Township)) 5 (4): 25–6.
39. Jones, Jessica. "Psychiatric Medication Risk in Children." Psych Central.com. June 10, 2010. Accessed September 23, 2014.

Medically Kidnapped

40. Smith M.D., Michael. "Marijuana vs. Alcohol: Compare Effects on the Body." WebMD. February 4, 2014.
41. Smith, C. M. "Origin and Uses of Primum Non Nocere—Above All, Do No Harm!" The Journal of Clinical Pharmacology: 371-77.
42. Gil, Eliana, PhD. "The California Child Abuse & Neglect Reporting Law Issues and Answers for Mandated Reporters." Rady Children's Hospital San Diego, 2012.
43. "Justina's Plea." YouTube. Accessed March 4, 2015. https://www.youtube.com/watch?v=20xv15LsVjw.
44. "The Case of Justina Pelletier Fact Sheet." Liberty Counsel, 2014. https://www.liberty.edu/media/9980/attachments/062714_Pelletier_Ti meline.pdf.
45. Frances, A. "The New Somatic Symptom Disorder in DSM-5 Risks Mislabeling Many People as Mentally Ill." BMJ: F1580.
46. Soloman, John. "Government Concludes Some AIDS Drug Experiments on Foster Child Violated Rules." Associated Press, June 5, 2005.
47. "Low White Blood Cell Count." Mayo Clinic. January 3, 2013. Accessed March 4, 2015.
48. Scheff, Liam. "Orphans on Trial." New York Press, July 1, 2004.

49. Orwell, George. Politics and the English Language. 1946.

Preparing for Court
50. "A Handbook for Parents and Guardians in Child Protection Cases : A Resource for Parents and Guardians: What You Need to Know about the Court Process." State Bar of Texas. Accessed September 23, 2014.
51. Arnold III, Thurman. "Pointers for Dealing with Family Court Judges (Difficult and Otherwise)—What Every Lawyer and Pro Per Should Know." Law Firm of Thurman Arnold. June 11, 2011.